To Catch a Cheat

To Catch a Cheat

The Insider's Guide
to Infidelity

Jim Richardson

Thorsons
An Imprint of HarperCollinsPublishers

Thorsons
An Imprint of HarperCollins*Publishers*
77–85 Fulham Palace Road,
Hammersmith, London W6 8JB

Published by Thorsons 1997
1 3 5 7 9 10 8 6 4 2

A catalogue record for this book
is available from the British Library

ISBN 0 7225 3466 3

Printed in Great Britain by Caledonian International Book
Manufacturing Ltd, Glasgow

'I have no data yet. It is a capital mistake to theorise before one has data. Insensibly one begins to twist facts to suit theories instead of theories to suit facts.'

Sherlock Holmes
from *A Scandal in Bohemia*, 1891

Author's Note

The author cannot be held responsible for the consequences of actions taken as a result of reading *To Catch a Cheat* and using the techniques therein. This publication is not suitable for persons under 16 years of age.

Contents

Acknowledgements

I would like to thank all the contributors to this book without whom it would not have been possible. The case study interviewees showed courage and honesty during our discussions.

I should also like to acknowledge the help of several private investigators, whose input was critical. For obvious reasons they would like to remain anonymous.

The police were instrumental in the corroboration of many of the details outlined in the case studies and for this I would like to expound my appreciation.

For their comments endorsing the psychological 'type' section, I would like to thank several professionals from the world of psychology.

Perhaps my last turn of gratitude should go to the person who helped the most, Samantha Noonan. Sam put herself in some unsavoury situations, gave up many of her valuable weekends, and left several heartbroken men standing outside restaurants to help in the research for *To Catch a Cheat*.

Introduction

Lancelot and Guinevere. Nelson and Lady Hamilton. Charles and Camilla. History and mythology are peppered with the stories of famous adulterers. For as long as people have sworn vows of fidelity they have broken them, seeking the forbidden thrill of sex with others.

Infidelity may be old news but it is big news if it happens to you. Trust lies at the heart of all human relationships. Trust is vital because it is so easy to break. Once broken, it is desperately hard to get back.

There is a potential cheat in all of us. However, cheats do not easily conform to recognisable 'stereotypes'. Whereas some behave as they do because of their circumstances or personality make-up, others are more calculating. They find it easy to justify their behaviour to themselves and lose sleep, not through guilt, but because they think they might be caught.

Many evolutionists believe that men are driven to be unfaithful by the genetic imperative to reproduce. A few thousand years of cultural evolution mean nothing in the face of millions of years of biological evolution. Society may say that untethered sexual desire is destructive but the body says have sexual intercourse as often and with as many individuals as possible.

Has there ever been a time when you desired a stranger sexually, even though you were quite happy within a relationship? I'll go out on a limb and say your answer will be a guilty 'yes'. Many of the men I interviewed toed the socially acceptable line whilst secretly nourishing highly promiscuous desires.

Not much has been written about infidelity. It remains a taboo subject. Everybody assumes their own relationship is immune to the possibility. If you are intrigued about this subject or perhaps even harbour suspicions about your own partner, however, this book is for you. It will help you understand some of the things that motivate a cheat, spot the tell-tale signs and use a range of techniques and finally confront the culprit.

Unless you catch them in bed it takes many pieces of hard evidence to make most cheats admit their guilt. I call this the 'shoplifter syndrome'. Ask any store detective to describe the behaviour of a shoplifter immediately after he has been caught and they will tell you of an individual who denies all. Even while the detective is emptying the stolen goods from the shoplifter's bag the thief will protest his innocence. Similarly a cheat is often unaware of the severity of his actions until he is found out. Denial is the only way to erase guilt as well as suspicion.

Cheating partners often have a lot more to lose than shoplifters by admitting their liability. Men will be aware of the financial penalties, the problem of access to their children and the breakdown of their official relationship – in that order! Little wonder then that denial is a knee-jerk reaction for any unfaithful male.

I know the mentality of the cheat only too well. During the '70s and '80s, I was a pathological sex addict. I chased women who could not have held a candle to the partners whom I was cheating upon. When the thrill of the chase ended in sexual conquest there was always a feeling of anti-climax. But this never deterred my pathological desire for sex.

I love women, I love sex and I love the excitement of the chase. But my infidelity was, I believe, born out of my experience – or lack of it – as a child. I spent most of my formative years in children's homes and with foster parents and never knew what it meant to have a family. I tried to fill the void by attention-seeking behaviour which infuriated care workers and foster parents alike. As an adult my insecurity led to a constant search for validation from women and my consequent infidelity.

I remember thinking, 'if only my partner knew…' and I began to think less of her for being so easily fooled. I have many regrets on that score. The cheat often starts to think this way and once he loses respect for his partner the relationship will inevitably break down. Several undeserving women suffered like this at my hands. Eventually I realised that, no matter how many women I slept with, my insecurity remained with me. It struck me too that our time on this earth is short and that I was wasting other people's lives. My behaviour was destructive on all levels.

I began talking to people about their views on and experiences of infidelity and a book began to emerge. There were 360 interviewees in all – those who had cheated and those who were cheated upon. Many of their stories were compelling in the extreme and I have used them (with names changed) as 'case studies' throughout the book. Often they are quoted at length to allow the reader to get into the minds of an array of love cheats. A few of the stories are quite bizarre. In no other aspect of life have I found the expression 'fact is stranger than fiction' to be more apt!

Should you be using this book to try to entrap an unfaithful partner I sincerely hope you will be one of the lucky ones whose suspicions prove to be unfounded. If they are not, I offer my deepest sympathies. This will rank as one of the most traumatic experiences of your life. But if curiosity leads you to read this book, I hope you will find the subject as eye-opening as I have.

This is how the book is organised. Chapter One introduces you to the problem of infidelity and to the personality of the cheat. How many people are actually unfaithful? What motivates them?

Chapter Two covers those tell-tale signs which show that something is amiss. Either your partner's behaviour is lacking in some way – they show what I call 'passive' signs – or they are exhibiting new and uncharacteristic behaviour – 'active' signs.

Chapter Three explains how the cheat will try to cover his tracks with an alibi. I will tell you how to test an alibi.

If the alibi doesn't hold water you will need to begin collecting hard evidence. You may have to verify bank details and credit card information, for example. I will tell you how to do this in Chapter Four.

Chapter Five looks at the most risky tactic for collecting hard evidence – following your partner. It also teaches you how to set traps for them.

The book concludes with a chapter on putting your evidence together. I then deal with the crucial business of confronting your cheating partner – the right way and the wrong way – and living with the aftermath.

A word of warning: the subject of infidelity often evokes the very worst in people. I found this during my research. Partners of people I interviewed began to view me with suspicion. On more than one occasion partners misconstrued things and thought I was involved in the affair. Consequently, I was physically attacked, sent threatening letters and subjected to several telephone hate campaigns. Luckily I lived to tell the tale!

A final note: I have written this book for men and women because both sexes cheat and are cheated upon. When I use 'he' or 'she' in the text it is for convenience only.

Chapter 1

Inside the Mind of a Cheat

Love cheats are not monsters. Under certain conditions any of us can be tempted to let attraction spill over into sexual intimacy. However certain kinds of cheats resemble each other, certain kinds of people become cheats and certain situations prompt infidelity. In this chapter I'll try to tell you how to recognise them.

But first some background. As I conducted my research I discovered that:

- Two out of three men and one out of three women admitted to having been unfaithful in their current relationship.

- All the men interviewed had cheated on a partner at some point during their life.

- Men tended to see infidelity as part and parcel of a relationship. Since many of their friends were all seeing other women they regarded emotional and sexual betrayal as 'normal'. In fact, many of the subjects interviewed expressed the view that being faithful was 'abnormal'.

- Most unfaithful men thought sex had very little to do with emotion; it was 'nothing personal', whether within or outside a relationship. To betray their partner sexually and emotionally was of no concern to them. They could have sex with a stranger and then return to the official relationship without regret or feelings of guilt.

- Several women I met shared the same mentality as male sex addicts. Far more however entered into the 'unfaithful partner' culture reluctantly.

The Unfaithful Male

Why are men unfaithful? And why do unfaithful men stay in relationships that are obviously cramping their style? Disturbingly, I found that most of them exhibited the same psychological characteristic as my former self – insecurity.

'Insecurity' is a broad term and I have not used it to give the cheat 'victim' status. Insecurity is no excuse for infidelity.

Peer pressure and society today demand that the average male should be seen in the company of a woman. Therefore many of my male interviewees maintained an apparently stable relationship just because that is what society deemed to be normal. They really were that shallow. They wanted to be in their stable relationships but they also wanted 'a bit on the side'.

Even within relationships men sometimes doubt their masculinity. They flex their 'libido muscles' by proving their sexual prowess with other women, an emphatic statement that they are male and proud.

So each conquest leads to a greater sense of self-worth? Not at all. The gratification gained is short-lived. Men tend to build their insecurity by their failures rather than bolstering their egos by noting conquests. I remember that it was the women who *shunned* my advances that affected me most.

I had to recognise my insecurity before I began to adopt a more mature outlook. Now I would rather be single than be in a relationship with someone who I know I would cheat upon. I also found that 'living a lie' was not all that it was cracked up to be. We must be true to ourselves and not waste another person's life.

I suggested to some of my unfaithful male interviewees that they had cheated because they were insecure.

Hostility and denial came my way. The '90s 'new man' was nowhere in sight. Men, it seems, were not kept on the straight and narrow by a dutiful partner who gave everything that they could want. Rather, this bored them. They saw infidelity as a way to try to inject a little spice into their lives.

To outline the many reasons why people cheat is beyond the scope of this book. Suffice it to say that an unstable family background affects our behaviour. (In men, it makes them more likely to cheat, whereas in women, it makes them more faithful in relationships.) Life events – such as the birth of a child, change of direction within a relationship by either party, or a mid-life crisis or the death of a parent – can precipitate cheating behaviour, but only if the inclination is essentially present.

The Unfaithful Female

A different attitude prevailed among the women I interviewed. They were almost always sorry to have entered into an affair. Many said how they were neglected emotionally and I couldn't help wondering how often this was because their partners were active cheats. The harder they tried to cultivate or rekindle a relationship the more they were repaid with indifference and rudeness.

The situation made them feel less feminine and grated against their sense of self-respect.

Given a choice of being single or remaining in a bad relationship, I found that women tended to opt for the bad relationship. Like men, they were often afraid of being alone, insecure and under social pressure to be in a 'couple'. However, if something was lacking in the official relationship and they found it with a new partner, they were more likely than men to leave their old partner unless children or money made it impossible.

Many of the women I spoke to had confronted a cheating partner with their suspicions but without any evidence. Inevitably this had backfired. The women's sincerity had not prompted the same response in their partner. In fact the more they had attacked their partners the more the men had protested their innocence. Those who tried an obliquer approach by saying 'we've got a problem within our relationship' fell at the first hurdle. To the men there wasn't a problem. They were doing exactly what they wanted and were getting away with it!

Unfaithful Types

So who are the cheats? My research has helped me to identify the following categories. I do not claim that these profiles are actual psychological 'types', but it may help you to determine whether your partner falls into one, none or several of the classifications.

The Sex Addict

The sex addict needs and is always interested in sex from any source, e.g. affairs, one night stands, prostitution and pornography. Their infidelity has no bearing on whether or not they love their partner. They separate sex from emotion and often lead a normal home life. Within minutes of having meaningless sex with a stranger they can return home to the 'official' relationship with no feelings of guilt or remorse. In fact in all other areas of the official relationship the sex addict can be extremely loyal. Given that he rarely believes he is wrong about anything and is often an accomplished liar, he is also very difficult to detect.

Sex addicts believe they are driven by the thrill of the chase. But, as I have already suggested, they actually hide feelings of inadequacy. They believe that if they can prove themselves desirable to others they will be valid in the eyes of the world.

Sex addicts only realise the true implications of their actions when they are caught. All of a sudden the thrill of the chase ceases to have any importance and they focus on the things that have real significance to them. Unfortunately, as soon as they feel secure within the relationship again, most forgiven sex addicts re-offend.

Jason, the subject of the following case study, is a self-confessed sex addict. Extreme as his behaviour is, he exhibits all the traits of his 'type'.

Jason (31) claims to have slept with more than 200 women in the course of his 13-year marriage to Sarah. He lost his job as a representative for a leading toy manufacturer because he chose to pursue women rather than to keep business appointments.

'My job as company representative called for a total commitment during my working hours. I remember driving to important meetings that could have earned the company thousands and spotting a good looking woman on the way there. Without a second thought I would stop the car and find an excuse to start chatting her up. I got lucky on more than one occasion.

'This did nothing for my professional standing. I would leave clients waiting at restaurants or hanging around my office. I could always find a good reason for being late or not turning up but eventually my manager had had enough and sacked me. Even while he was telling me I found myself wanting him to hurry up and send me packing because I had been flirting with a girl who worked in a nearby shop that morning and I wanted to go back and finish the job!

'Sarah went crazy when I told her the news. She saw no reason why I should have been sacked. She would see me going to work each morning, and assumed that all those late night meetings with clients should have earned me a rise! Even though she knew I liked women, she just didn't have a clue about the real me.

'Even when we'd just met and I went round to her flat for dinner I seduced her flatmate, Harriet, because Sarah had been called away for family reasons! After we were married I had sex with my friend's wives and girlfriends, my female work colleagues and prostitutes in Amsterdam where the boys and I used to go on trips. I tried it on with any woman who was attractive to me.'

Then Jason met Debbie, some 10 years his junior. For four months he found excuses to get away from his wife to see her. Eventually he decided to come clean and move in with her. He even thought Debbie was the answer to his philandering ways.

'Sarah wasn't at all surprised when I moved out. I was taken aback when she said she wasn't blind or stupid and had seen me several times with other women.

'Deb's dad was loaded and had bought her a lovely flat in an exclusive area of London. She began introducing me to her high society friends. They were all gorgeous and I fancied them from the start. Two weeks after I moved in Debbie had to go on a work conference for a week. I had already taken a shine to

one of her friends, Sally. Whilst Debbie was away
I invited her round and we ended up making love.
One month later I left Debbie for Sally.'

It only took a week for Jason to end up in
bed with Sally's sister Katie, claiming that she
had seduced him. He fled the scene, homeless and
friendless. Since sex had ruined his life he decided
to give it up for a while. After living at his mother's
for six months he has found a new job and will soon
be moving into a new flat.

'I still see Katie from time to time but she tells
me that she could never get really involved with me
because I am not to be taken seriously! I suppose I
deserve that. I cannot justify the way I treated my
wife and the other women. All I can say is that
something took over whenever I saw a girl I found
attractive. I was risking a lot of things but none
seemed remotely important compared with the
temptation I could see in front of me.

The Opportunist

The Opportunist is different to the Sex Addict in one vital
respect – he does not *actively* seek out sexual partners. He

is a relatively faithful mate but will succumb to advances from others or encouragement from peers, especially if they are sex addicts. He is vulnerable in social situations, especially when his resolve is lessened by alcohol.

The impressionable nature of opportunists puts them at risk of becoming emotionally involved with their new partners. They are not compulsive cheats but may reoffend if they got away with infidelity before.

Tanya had been going out with Mike for almost a year but during the last two months she felt he was losing interest.

One Friday night she was walking into town with her friends Tracey and Lisa when a car pulled up beside them. Inside were three of their ex-boyfriends – Jason, Alan and Nick – whom they hadn't seen for about a year. They said they had just moved into a flat round the corner and invited the three girls round.

When they got there they all started talking and drinking. Soon they were pretty drunk. Alan paired off with Tracey and Nick with Lisa. Tracey describes how a mixture of factors led her to consider pairing off with Jason. She was drunk, but this didn't impair her judgement. There was considerable peer pressure, especially when the rest of her friends (all of whom were now in new relationships) disappeared off to the bedrooms. And she still had feelings for Jason.

But she claims the main factor was that Mike had been paying her no attention of late. She wanted to be 'loved' and 'pampered' and 'flattered'. Jason was doing all of that – telling her how beautiful she was, how much he'd missed her and so forth. She says she knew it was all 'flannel' to get her into bed, but she didn't care. All the factors together made it 'impossible' for her to say no, she says.

When she saw Mike the next day she felt utterly guilty and finished their relationship there and then. She saw Jason a few times but realised she'd made a mistake. After confessing all to Mike, they got back together.

The Romantic

There are two different faces to the Romantic. The true romantic will usually leave his official partner for the new love of his life. The Romantic cheat, however, loves the buzz of romance and seeing someone showing him intense, emotional commitment.

But the truth is that the Romantic cheat will never give any real commitment. Romantics are driven by fantasy and idealism and may well sweep you off your feet at the beginning of the relationship. Once the excitement lessens and reality sets in they go elsewhere in search of the same feelings.

Romantics are little more than con artists who play the part of people in love and are more concerned with the superficial side of romance. They love the smooth caddish image they often cultivate for themselves. They are emotionally mercenary, leading on unsuspecting, trusting victims before dumping them. Romantics are quite easily detected as their lifestyle calls for meetings in hotels, expensive dinners and gifts, all of which must be paid for and therefore registered.

One of my interviewees caught out her boyfriend of 10 months when she began to suspect that he was having a 'bit on the side'. Her doubts arose when he started paying less and less attention to her, and continually disappeared on 'business', refusing to give her a contact telephone number.

She eventually discovered that she was herself the 'bit on the side' and that her partner was in fact married with two children.

The Perfectionist

When the Perfectionist becomes unsatisfied with his 'official' relationship, rather than having the courage to confront the problems or end the relationship, he looks elsewhere to fill in the gaps.

Perfectionists are striving for the perfect relationship but, when they realise they cannot get all of it from one person, they involve several people.

Matthew had been having an affair for several months. Carol, Matthew's wife, had caught him by using a technique outlined later in this book. Matthew initially decided to leave Carol for his lover Paula. However, several months later, Matthew began to call Carol telling her he had made a big mistake and needed time to deal with his problems.

One afternoon Matthew turned up at Carol's house and began to cry in front of her. She hugged him and asked him if he was still with Paula. Sheepishly he said he was but that they were no longer having sex. Did Paula know he had come round to talk to her or that they were trying to get back together, asked Carol. 'No,' said Matthew, 'but then she never understood me the way you do.'

At that Carol threw him out of the house and told him never to call her again. She believes that Matthew wanted the best of both worlds. He should have left Paula before approaching her if he genuinely wanted a reconciliation.

While Matthew was having the affair, Paula gave him the thrill of being a 'naughty boy' whilst Carol provided the stability. Later, however, Matthew became excited at the prospect of having a return affair with his own wife because Paula had become the established woman in his life. Sure enough, six months later (and after their divorce was finalised) Carol heard that Matthew was to marry his lover. At the time there was talk of him having another affair with his lover's best friend and indeed some time later Matthew left Paula for this other woman.

Some men see constant turmoil in their relationships as a perfect state. In the above case study, Matthew was looking for his ultimate relationship: one which saw him in turmoil with his official partner whilst having a mistress on the periphery. Causing havoc in his personal life made Matthew feel in control.

However, when Carol threw him out, the control element was taken away from him. At that point Matthew felt uncomfortable and tried to regain his 'happy' status quo. When this proved impossible, he played out his perfect relationship script with his mistress.

The Attention Seeker

The Attention Seeker has low self-esteem and looks for reassurance in the arms of another. Attention Seekers feel they are not getting the support they need from their partners and so turn to other available people. Sex is usually less important to them but they still use it to convince themselves they are receiving the attention they deserve.

It is easy to take advantage of Attention Seekers because all they really need is someone to talk to. Perhaps they are finding it hard to cope with a difficult situation in their life.

Attention Seekers usually admit to their infidelity as they tend to feel guilt and regret.

The Accident

An Accident can happen to the most faithful of partners. The subject is usually living quite happily, harbouring no thoughts of unfaithfulness. Then a friendship or work relationship progresses to the point of emotional and sexual involvement.

Guilt will be a major issue for the accidental cheat and you can expect them to be giving out plenty of the passive and active signals described in Chapter Two.

We can pity this kind of cheat but cannot wholly sympathise with them. Remember – there are *no* real Accidents in infidelity!

The following story sees a joke turn into 'accidental' infidelity:

_____

Barbara (28) met Simon (33) through a friend at a party. Barbara's identical twin sister Sharon (28) lived with her boyfriend Carl (24) and they planned to marry.

One night Barbara couldn't make a date with Simon. She couldn't reach him by telephone, so she telephoned her sister, Sharon – who lived just round the corner from Simon – to ask her to go to his flat with a message.

When Sharon arrived Simon assumed that she was Barbara. 'Come on then!' he said as he took her arm and ran down the road. Sharon thought she would play along 'for a laugh'.

The hilarity continued on into the pub where Simon bought the drinks. Sharon had already carried the joke further than she had planned, but by now she was enjoying herself. She admits that she found Simon attractive.

They were quite drunk when they left the pub and headed for Simon's flat. Here they made love. Sharon left at midnight leaving Simon still blissfully unaware of the deception.

Sharon couldn't sleep that night and decided to tell Barbara everything when she next saw her. She was sure that the truth would eventually come out anyway. She decided to confront the two of them together that evening, when Barbara was planning to see Simon at his flat.

When she arrived it was obvious that neither of them had cottoned on to the previous evening's events. She took fright and backed out of her plan. After all, it was a one off and, as long as they remained ignorant, surely nobody would get hurt.

Unfortunately Sharon later found herself to be pregnant and she was convinced that the baby was Simon's. Carl was Italian whilst Simon was a red-headed Scot, so she began to worry that the baby would be born with red hair!

Sharon was still agonising over how to handle the situation when, six weeks later, Barbara announced that she and Simon had decided to marry because Barbara had become pregnant too. She asked Sharon and Carl if they wanted to get married at the same time.

Finally Sharon plucked up courage to tell Barbara what had happened. She explained how Simon had not realised but, understandably, Barbara went crazy. She didn't believe that her husband-to-be could mistake her sister for her. Worst of all was the news that Sharon was possibly carrying Simon's child.

Barbara took her feelings out on Simon, treating him coldly. When Sharon told Carl what had happened he left her that same evening.

Months later, when Sharon's baby was born, it was quite obviously Carl's. Somehow the bond created between them by their child seemed to improve things. Carl moved back in with her although they didn't get married. Barbara eventually married Simon and they have a small son.

Of course, most of my interviewees failed to conform exactly to one of the types I have described above. However they all fell within the broad spectrum, with the Sex Addict at one end of the scale and the Accident at the other. Those who tended towards sexual addiction exhibited traits of the Opportunist and Romantic cheat but were least likely to be involved in an accidental encounter.

Those who had cheated on their partner by 'accident' were much less likely to show the traits of an addict but, nevertheless, held the potential to travel in this direction. I would have placed myself somewhere near the Sex Addict end of the scale while exhibiting characteristics found in the Opportunist and Romantic. There were few accidents for me…

The Cheating Type

You can't help who you are attracted to, but many unfaithful 'types' could be detected in the early days of a relationship if only we could recognise the tell-tale signs.

The First Time You Meet...

He is very attentive as he plays his opening gambit, looking you in the eye and smiling his sewn-in smile. After the first drink, however, he will be talking to you but looking at every woman who passes by.

He talks about you for five minutes before reverting to his favourite subject – himself.

He lies, perhaps confiding in you that he doesn't usually come to places like this while appearing to know all the staff by name.

He says he is shy with girls while slipping his hand around your waist and talking about sex in an explicit manner.

A stranger (usually another woman) approaches you when he goes to the bathroom and tells you to be careful.

Over the Following Weeks...

He forgets your name, or worse, he calls you by another name. Some cheats find it safer to use generic expressions: 'babe', 'darling', 'honey' and the like.

He can't give you his home telephone number and 'because he is a secret agent', he can't give you his work number either. You have seen his address book in his jacket pocket but he has written your number on

the back of a cigarette packet. He is always sloping off
to make telephone calls. His mobile telephone is always
switched off when he is with you.

He always has a reason for leaving in the early hours.
However, he never invites you back to his place.

After seeing you for four nights in succession, suddenly he can only 'fit you in' for an hour between six and seven
on a Wednesday evening. And no, he can't spend New
Year's Eve with you because he has promised to 'baby-sit
for his grandmother'. He never introduces you to his
friends and family.

The best indicator of all is your own intuition. If your
gut feeling is that your new lover is too good to be true,
then he probably is. But if the relationship continues,
you'll need evidence!

Chapter 2

The Cheat's Behaviour

H e's not the man he was.' 'We don't seem to talk any more.' Unless your unfaithful partner has the sensitivity of an amoeba he will be experiencing a wide range of conflicting emotions. His excitement at his new affair will usually be more than balanced by feelings of frustration, confusion and even (if you are lucky) some guilt.

This chapter describes the changes in behaviour you might expect to see in your partner when he or she is being unfaithful. I have divided them into 'passive' and 'active' signals. Passive signals are often subconscious in origin. Your partner will react in a negative fashion towards aspects of day-to-day life. Active signals are more obvious and derive from the conscious reactions of the cheat towards the situation they have created.

When the unofficial relationship is new and there is no pressure upon the cheat he will usually give out passive signals. Active signals come later, can be explosive and are more likely to bring the situation to a head.

However obvious any of these signals may be in your partner, they do not provide enough proof to enable you to confront them. You will also need some of the hard evidence described in Chapter Four.

Before we proceed, I must urge caution. If you begin to have genuine suspicions about your partner you can expect to feel some of the most destructive and life-altering emotions – jealousy, hatred, self-pity and desire for retribution. This is not a game or a soap opera.

Ask yourself these questions:

- Am I being balanced about the situation?

- Do I really want to know more?

- Why do I want to know?

- If I find out that my partner is being unfaithful, how will it affect me and my relationship?

- Do I want to create a situation that might cause the relationship to end?

- Am I strong enough to cope with finding my part-ner with another man/woman?

Gathering Evidence

If your suspicions are aroused by the signals I am about
to describe and you decide to embark on an investigation, read *all* of the book first. Then equip yourself with
the dossier described at the start of Chapter Three and
prepare in the first instance to be an observer.

You may encounter some unpleasant situations
but, equally, you should not become paranoid about
your partner. Try to remain calm and do not under
any circumstances explode at them, however upset
you may feel. Do not resort to anything you might
regret once time has had the chance to work its
healing effect.

Remember – crucially – that no one piece of information should be taken as absolute proof. Perhaps your
partner is secretly helping out a friend in an embarrassing
situation. Perhaps they are generous with the lifts they
give to their friends and colleagues. Perhaps they are discreetly planning a treat for you!

Passive Signals

Passive signals are a minefield of ambiguity. At best
they offer circumstantial rather than solid evidence
of infidelity. There are many reasons why a subject
may not want sex, a cuddle, or even to talk. If your
emotional state is genuine they will need your support
and understanding, not your suspicious questioning.
Be discreet!

Lack of Emotional Expression

Most couples have a repertoire of signs of affection.
These mean a lot in the context of the relationship,
however inconspicuous. Kissing before leaving for work,
sitting beside each other when watching the television,
picking each other up on arrival at a station or airport,
making love even when life is stressful – perhaps even
'scheduling' it.

If your partner is usually an affectionate individual
it is easy to see when something is lacking. However, not
all human beings express emotions easily.

You should assume that your partner's character
change is the result of depression or stress. You should
not jump to conclusions. Can you ask them – tactfully
and sympathetically – what is wrong? Only when you

have ruled out other reasons should you consider the possibility of infidelity.

Lack of Sex Drive

If your partner is showing a lack of interest in sex it may be that they are being satisfied elsewhere. But remember that 1) sex drive tends to dwindle with the years; 2) it is quite normal for men and women to oscillate between sexual activity and inactivity; 3) stress, depression or an undiagnosed illness can all cause lack of interest in sex.

It is worth pointing out too, however, that our desire for excitement does not wane. Many people can exhibit near celibacy at home whilst being highly sexed in the company of others.

Lack of Communication

You don't see much of your partner. When you do, they slump down in front of the television and communicate only in grunts.

If your partner has stopped talking to you – sharing the day's goings on, their thoughts, ideas, dreams and desires – it could be a sign that they have found another confidant.

If you have suspicions, do not act rashly. Simply ask your partner the reason for their lack of conversation and record their answers.

Lack of Eye Contact

Does your partner have trouble looking you in the eye? The three recognised reasons for this are low self-esteem, depression and dishonesty. Decide which is most likely to be the case in your partner.

Active Signals

Active signals are more substantial as they call for some new effort from your partner.

Keep records!

Mood Swings

Your partner has been interacting with you in a manner that is familiar to you. But suddenly something trivial – maybe a broken appliance or perceived injustice – makes

them crazy with anger at you or at life in general. Are
you unsure of your partner's mood from one moment
to another?

Or is their anger more persistent – blaming you for the
problems within the relationship, accusing you of wasting
their life, insulting your character or sexual prowess? Does
it lead to aggressive behaviour?

Perhaps these are familiar scenarios. If not, they
could indicate emotional turmoil. Are the mood swings
and aggressive behaviour inflicted on other friends and
family too? If they are saved for you it could indicate that
your partner is having an affair and is resentful towards
you for 'being in the way'.

After the 'honeymoon' period, the excitement of the
early days in a relationship may wane. If your partner has
begun an affair they will be experiencing anew the emotional highs and sexual excitement of a new relationship.
Their official relationship will seem boring, ordinary,
moribund. This is not your fault but rather the fault of an
immature, unrealistic and selfish partner.

Sexual Activity

You occasionally refuse sex, perhaps saying you have
the proverbial 'headache'. This usually leads to a mild
confrontation, but not tonight. Your partner rolls over and
falls asleep, not at all perturbed.

Similarly he may complain about the way you perform in bed, suffer from impotence, or, on the con-
trary, try new and unexpected sexual acts with you.

These are all signs that can give your partner away
if they are having a sexual relationship elsewhere.

As we've already seen, some individuals are sex
addicts. Should your partner fall into this category you
may have a problem detecting them, as any sexual activity
they are involved in elsewhere may not affect their sexual
relationship with you.

Personal Appearance

Has your partner recently purchased new clothes, had an
unusually expensive haircut, joined a gym, or improved
their appearance in some other way?

There is nothing wrong with this in principle but, if
the two of you are not getting on as well as you'd like, it
could indicate that your partner is looking elsewhere for
all that a healthy relationship yields.

Personal Hygiene

Should your partner rush into the shower when they return home or feel the need to wash and change before kissing you 'hello' – be suspicious!

An unusual interest in personal cleanliness could signal a change of allegiance in their intimate relationships.

If your partner returns home from a night out with the girls or lads and gets into bed as sweet smelling as when they left, you would be right to question the situation. Where can you get a shower on a night out and, more important, why would you?

In the following case study a cheating husband shows several active signals of his infidelity that lead his wife to the truth.

―――――――――

Kevin (32) had been married to Joanne (27) for three years. Joanne was very friendly with neighbours Andrea (30) and Tracie (24) who lived either side of her. Neither Andrea or Tracie had men in their lives and would spend long hours in Joanne's home gossiping.

One afternoon Andrea asked Kevin over to fix her son's bike. She had always been attracted to him and that afternoon found herself flirting outrageously. Kevin did not hesitate to respond.

Kevin began seeing Andrea whenever he could. He would leave for work in the morning and sneak next door to make love to Andrea. He would arrive two hours late at the video shop where he worked, giving lame excuses about traffic and sick children. As if his life wasn't complicated enough, he soon started an affair with his other neighbour.

Tracie worked part-time in the video shop and had problems with her six year-old son. As Kevin was a good listener they would talk for hours about her situation. This led to an affair which Kevin and Tracie conducted mostly at the video shop, making love there when the store was closed.

Perversely, Andrea and Tracie continued to visit Kevin's wife Joanne every afternoon for coffee.

Joanne began to suspect Kevin of having an affair when he started trying to improve his appearance for no particular reason. He bought new clothes at a time when they couldn't afford to pay the bills, joined a gym and started trying to colour his few grey hairs. Ironically Joanne had suggested that he do this several months before but Kevin had just laughed, saying that the grey hair made him look 'respectable'.

Joanne told her two best friends, Andrea and Tracie, of her fears. Both listened in sympathy, unaware that Kevin was not just cheating on Joanne but on the two of them as well.

Gradually the horror of the situation began to dawn on Joanne and her suspicions lighted upon Tracie first. One afternoon Kevin came in from work smelling of Tracie's perfume. Joanne decided to watch his movements. In the course of several morning surveillance sessions Joanne observed some strange behaviour on Kevin's part. Every day he would pretend to go to work, getting into his car and driving to the end of the street. Then, instead of turning right towards his workplace, he would turn left and then double back on himself by taking the next left. He would park and sneak around the corner to Andrea's house. As he reached the house he would get down on all fours before crawling on his belly into Andrea's back garden and into her back door!

Joanne had assumed that Kevin's affair was with Tracie and she describes how confused she was the first time she witnessed his odd behaviour. However she decided to confront them. When she burst through the back door she found Kevin and Andrea in a state of undress. Kevin lamely tried to explain that he and Andrea were planning a surprise party for her. Joanne kicked Kevin and started to batter Andrea.

At this point Tracie entered the fray. She had heard the commotion and, when she entered, knew at once what had happened. She attacked Kevin.

Joanne then attacked Tracie too and they all ended in a heap on the floor.

The truth emerged and Kevin went missing for a week. When he returned he found his clothes had been burnt and the remains were on the front lawn. Joanne divorced Kevin and moved away from the area soon after. Andrea doesn't speak to Tracie any longer. Kevin has moved in with Tracie.

———————————

The Sudden Change of Attitude

Has your partner recently started to take a new interest in you and your home life together? This is not necessarily a cause for concern as it is quite normal for people to try to put a little fizz back into a sagging relationship.

Perhaps they want to rekindle some of the initial excitement you felt; perhaps they think you've been taking each other for granted; maybe they simply want to show you some genuine care and attention. You will have to decide.

On the flip side, it could be that your partner is cheating on you and is feeling guilty or in danger of being caught out. They may be acting out a 'double bluff' thinking that, if they are particularly attentive to you, you will never suspect that something is amiss.

Your partner may also be unnerved to discover their sense of security being undermined. Many individuals find this in their relationship with a regular, official partner who is to them a safety blanket – a convenient retreat when their new lover is not around or when their fling isn't going to plan. Every so often they nurture this stable relationship to ensure that it will still be there when it is required.

If the affair is an intense one, your partner may even be under pressure from their lover to leave you. It is unlikely that your partner wants this, at least in the early stages of the romance. By pampering you and building up their official relationship they can easily choose later to drop their lover.

Their new-found 'commitment' to you also gives them a great excuse not to leave you and to force their lovers – in a cowardly fashion – to make the break if that is destined to happen. When forced to decide between two people, most cheats – particularly men – will choose the safe option.

Misreading the Evidence

In the following case study Emma concluded that her boyfriend John's passive and active signals were strong evidence that he was having an affair, when the truth was in fact far more difficult to fathom.

John (24) had lived with several girls in the past and was regarded as a bit of a cad. He was seeing Emma (22) when he found a new obsession.

Emma had known John for almost four years and their relationship had begun some six months before the events described.

One afternoon John visited his local paper shop for some cigarettes and picked up a raunchy Sunday newspaper. He had never purchased one before and thought it would cause amusement at the pub. John never reached the pub that night nor indeed for any night over the following 11 months.

John found the provocative images of nude women more exciting than he ever dreamed possible. They turned him on more than real sex. Over the next few days he graduated from daily papers to top-shelf soft porn magazines. He began to buy new magazines as often as possible but tired of them after only one browse through. The obsession took over his life.

He became moody and hostile towards Emma, who began to feel that she was in the way when she went to see John at his flat. She found it particularly disturbing that he couldn't make eye contact with her.

By the end of the first month, John had dipped into his savings and spent several hundred pounds on magazines. He describes how he began to fantasise about women in the street and how he began to see them only as 'bums' and 'tits' to be ogled at.

John became so engrossed in pornographic images that he stopped feeling the need for a real girlfriend. One evening Emma called to see John at his flat and was turned away at the door. She began to suspect he was seeing someone else and confronted him. John laughed and told Emma that this was the last thing he was thinking about. He suddenly became quite serious and began to tell her of his worry that he was becoming addicted to something.

Emma continued to shout at John and reiterated her belief that he was being unfaithful. She now regrets her reaction as she believes he was actually trying to ask her for help. As it was she told John to call her in a few days to sort things out once and for all. John did not call Emma for the next 10 months.

The only thing that kept John in employment was his need for the money to finance his addiction to ever more graphic pornographic material. He worked with heavy machinery and needed to be 'on the ball' at all times. One afternoon his mind was so full of pornographic images and thoughts of where his next 'hit' was coming from that he neglected the vital safety rules at work. He should have been watching a piece of steel in a pressing machine. The man who removed each piece relied on John to keep the heavy press out of his way. On this occasion it came down a little too soon and crushed his colleague's forearm. The accident could easily have proved fatal.

John's addiction progressed to pornographic films. His hunger for these was worse than it had been for the magazines and took its toll financially and socially. He stopped seeing his family and friends and showed no interest in real women. He lost weight and let himself go. On the rare occasions he did see his friends he would talk only about pornography.

Emma saw John's friends at their local pub one evening and heard that he had become a recluse. She realised she had been wrong about John's fidelity to her and was sure he had become a drug addict. She enlisted the help of his friends who, one afternoon, talked him into going for a drink. He got very drunk and they took him home.

When they entered John's flat they couldn't believe the scene that confronted them. They were appalled at John's flat. It had become a shrine to pornography. The walls and even the windows were covered in pages from magazines. There was no daylight in any of the rooms and piles of pornographic magazines covered the floors. Around the television, 80 –100 X-rated movies were piled up. Fast food wrappings, dirty plates, cups and clothes were strewn everywhere.

While John slept off the alcohol his friends cleaned the flat. When John awoke he was visibly shaken to see this. However, when questioned by one of his friends who telephoned later that evening, he admitted his problem and for the first time in months enquired about Emma.

Later he called her and said he had never been physically unfaithful to her. His addiction to pornography had taken away his sense of reality. Emma went straight round to John's flat and they hugged each other. She assumed they would get back together there and then but discovered that John had become physically and emotionally dysfunctional with 'real' women.

John explained his addiction to Emma and she felt that, in a manner of speaking, he had been unfaithful to her. He had chosen celluloid bimbos over someone who loved and cared for him.

Eventually, however, she had to admit that he hadn't actually been unfaithful to her in the traditional sense of the word.

To this day John can only look at a woman in sexual terms. He still finds it impossible to interact in an intimate way with another human being. His relationship with Emma is only a friendship. Emma believes that she could have helped John more when he initially asked for help. She doesn't know if she will stay with John but for now plans to help him as much as possible. John is currently seeing a psychologist.

Chapter 3

The Alibi

All those familiar with television police shows will know how important an alibi is to a defendant's case. A case can stand or fall on its reliability. The use of an alibi puts a would-be cheat in their most vulnerable position because they will be telling a story that can be disproved by one little mistake.

So this is the point at which you can really start to get your teeth into some detection work. A seasoned cheat will have an elaborate web of friends and excuses with which they create their alibis.

This chapter covers the types of alibi a cheat will employ and introduces you to the methods by which you may be able to prove or disprove them.

But first a little preparation is in order.

Gathering Evidence

Buy yourself an exercise book. This will be your 'evidence dossier' – the most important weapon in your fight to find the truth. The whole system is designed around the premise that 'a liar needs a good memory'. If you use your dossier properly the resulting data will be impossible to challenge. The format detailed here has been designed to retain only the most important information and to maintain consistency. It is vital that you follow it. This is a good example of one that works:

Incident Report

Alibi Details

Date of incident _____ Time of incident _____

Weather conditions _____

Area location(s) _____

_____

_____

_____

Names given by your partner _____

_____

_____

_____

Addresses given _____

_____

_____

_____

_____

_____

Telephone numbers given _____

_____

_____

Your partner's story/excuse _____

_____

_____

_____

_____

_____

Evidence that your partner puts forward to back their alibi

_____

_____

Your Findings

Where your partner's story matches your findings or the
information is non-applicable, just mark OK. Do *not*
leave blank spaces!

Date of incident _____ Time of incident _____

Inconsistencies regarding weather _____
_____

Location discrepancy _____
_____
_____

Names that don't match up   1) _____
2) _____
3) _____
4) _____

Address discrepancies   1) _____
_____
2) _____
_____
3) _____
_____
4) _____
_____
_____

Telephone numbers that did or did not appear on phone
bills or were falsely given   1) _____
2) _____
3) _____
4) _____

Inconsistencies in your partner's alibi _____

_____

_____

Hard evidence disproving your partner's alibi _____

_____

_____

_____

Bank account/credit card details _____

_____

Car check/clothes search _____

_____

Telephone evidence _____

_____

_____

Mystery telephone numbers _____

_____

_____

Trap evidence _____
_____
_____

Miscellaneous _____
_____
_____
_____

Circumstantial evidence (e.g. passive/active signals)
_____
_____
_____
_____
_____
_____
_____
_____

Do not forget to attach hard evidence, such as receipts and bank records, to each relevant incident report.

Devote a whole page of A4 paper to a single incident. The top half of each page is for the information given by your partner. It is the equivalent of a police incident report. Write down the details of the alibi as soon as possible to avoid vagueness or inaccuracy. Be sure to include notes on your partner's behaviour and their comments concerning the alibi. Try to keep your entries factual and as easy to follow as possible. Remember, it may be some months before you return to a given entry – you will need to understand it without ambiguity.

Note down the following information:

• The date on which the incident occurred.

• The weather conditions prevalent during the suspect period (*see 'car checking' in Chapter Four*).

• The time given by your partner for the suspect incident.

• The alleged whereabouts of your partner. If they have been in several different locations, add the approximate time at which they claim to have been in each.

• Names your partner includes in their alibi, including friends, relatives, helpful strangers. If no name is given, enter the person's function in the alibi (e.g. AA man or pub landlord).

• Addresses given. If unavailable, give approximate locations.

• All phone numbers from which your partner claims to have called.

- Your partner's version of events. Write only the facts. Do not embellish their story with your interpretation. Keep it simple.

The half page below each incident report is for your cross references and for other evidence that may come to light long after the event described at the top of the page took place, including your remarks on inconsistencies. This will be explained further in the final chapter.

If you can afford it, you should also buy yourself a voice activated cassette recorder. This can be purchased at any high street electrical store. An ordinary tape recorder can also be used but the recording time is greatly reduced.

The techniques described in the book are not illegal. Though you may modify them to suit your needs, take care not to render yourself open to prosecution by practising them in a criminal manner. Consult a solicitor if you are unsure.

The Non-Verifiable Alibi

'The car broke down. I was miles from anywhere. I couldn't contact you.'

The most successful alibi is one that does not rely on other people, cannot be rumbled by some form of receipt or ticket and which makes clear sense given the subject's particular lifestyle. All you can do in these instances is ask your partner for a lot of detail without appearing to interrogate them. Keep a record. The cheat will have to remember everything they said and corroborate it when you ask them again days or weeks later!

Perhaps your partner claims to have broken down miles from anywhere. How did they get back?; how long did it take?; what was the weather like?; did anyone stop to help?

Whenever the car is part of an alibi, check it afterwards. If it broke down in a field or ditch and it was raining, look for mud and grass on the wheels and mud flaps. The driver would have got mud on their boots too so check for muddy marks inside the car. Did they have anyone with them in the car? Check for signs of someone having been in the passenger seat. Look in the ashtray for unusual wrappers or cigarette butts.

If your partner claims to have called a breakdown recovery service you can verify their alibi. Some breakdown organisations will provide details of all call-outs on a member's car in the form of a statement. To access

this information, however, you must be named on the
membership. Other organisations are more cautious
with such information as they may be contravening
the Data Protection Act. No motoring organisation
will give details over the telephone.

Your partner says he couldn't contact you. Sorry, not
true. Most breakdown services offer to call the family or
friends of the stranded party.

As you will find out in Chapter Four, you can also corroborate your partner's alibi by checking their bank statement or credit card bill. Whatever evidence you find, write
it down!

If your partner claims they have been calling you
on the telephone all night ('there must be a fault on the
line'), check with the operator. Or, if you live in Britain,
dial 1471 and you will hear the number and time of the
last call made to your phone number. The area code will
tell you exactly where the caller was and may help either
to prove or disprove your partner's story. This won't work
of course if the caller phoned through a company telephone network or dialled 141 before your number
because they did not want their call traced! If you live
elsewhere, check with your local phone company to see
if a comparable service is on offer.

There are a million and one alibis a cheat can offer.
But if they give you one that is impossible to corroborate,
this is in itself suspicious, particularly if they are vague
about certain points. Use your common sense. Take the
alibi apart, checking every minor detail.

Work as an Alibi

'Working late' has almost become a cliché for infidelity
in popular culture. But it is one of the most frequent
ruses. Is your partner going out for drinks with colleagues after work more than usual? Or are they
increasingly absent from the office during the day?
It may well be that they are not doing the kind of
work they say!

You have many ways of determining the truth of
the 'working late' excuse.

Find out why they needed to work on that particular night or weekend. If they are going to be working
late again, ask for a telephone number you can call in
an emergency – and not for a mobile phone! If they
make an excuse, question why.

If your partner is paid by the hour you can check
wage slips, time sheets and salary details to determine
when the extra hours (if there are any) were clocked up.

An excellent way to gather information is to use
unwitting informers. Call your partner's work friends/
colleagues on the pretence, for example, that you are
arranging a surprise party. In this situation you can
ask many legitimate questions about your partner's
movements and work routine. Ultimately you can
tell your informers that the party idea fell through.
This has the advantage of secrecy – none of your

partner's colleagues will want to 'spoil the surprise'. They are spying on their colleague with the best of intentions.

You may be tempted to visit your partner's workplace. Before you choose this option, think hard about it. You will need a very good reason and you must make the visit seem inconsequential. And this is the worst place to create a scene.

If you do decide to go, pretend that you noticed they had been working a bit too hard and decided to treat them to a surprise meal in a restaurant. If your partner is not at work when you get there – why? Return home and do not mention that you were at your partner's workplace. Instead, ask probing questions to determine whether they claim to have been at work all day.

If they are at work when you arrive, note how they react to your surprise arrival? Do they greet you with a warm hug and genuine pleasure or are they shocked and flustered?

———————————

Julie (28) had been married to Alan (31) for six years. They had no children and owned a house in a London suburb. Julie worked at a top legal firm in the City whilst Alan was a technical designer who worked from home.

At one point Julie started to come home later than usual from work. She said that she was over-worked and that she couldn't possibly do all that was required of her during the day. She told Alan that she would have to start working late to get through the backlog.

As Alan worked from home he would usually prepare their evening meal. Over the next seven weeks he became accustomed to Julie calling him around 4pm to tell him that she would be working late and that he should eat without her. So he began calling her after working hours to see how she was getting on. On several occasions Toby, a work colleague, answered the phone. Alan couldn't help wondering why he was always there when Julie was working.

Alan casually asked two of Julie's friends (who were also work colleagues) about work procedures and why there appeared to be such an excess of work in Julie's department. They didn't seem to know what Alan was talking about. He also asked them about Toby and why he was working late too. Again the women seemed confused. One of them told Alan that Toby worked in a different depart-ment so he shouldn't even be in the same office as her after work.

The next day Alan called Julie's company and asked to be put through to Toby's department. Just before the company operator put him through she said, 'Toby White? Yes sir, that's the International Law department. Hold on.' Alan put the phone down. Now he knew for sure that Toby didn't work in the same department as Julie.

When Julie returned home that night Alan confronted her with his findings. For a while Julie denied all, but eventually she broke down and told Alan that she had started an affair with Toby six weeks before. She had created her own problems with her workload so that she would be forced to work for an extra half an hour. Then she and Toby would spend the remaining 1–2 hours in the (now deserted) office 'getting to know each other'.

With counselling and a lot of hard work, Julie and Alan climbed the steep slope of reconciliation. Julie realised that something was lacking in her relationship with Alan and that it was this, and not the buzz of a little romance with Toby, that was the cause of her indiscretion. Alan and Julie are happy now but Julie left the job she loved to cut the final link with the scene of her infidelity.

Friends

Using a friend to corroborate a false alibi can be hazardous for the cheat as it calls for lies to be remembered by two people.

Friends will generally provide alibis for a certain period of time but I have found that they soon become uncomfortable – intellectually or morally – with the situation. They end up advising the cheat to look for alibis elsewhere. The exception is when they need a reciprocal service from your partner!

If your partner claims to be visiting or socialising with one particular friend for some weeks or months and then repeats this procedure with others, it may be that each friend in turn is allowing themselves to be used as an alibi until they prove resistant.

Does your partner give false alibis for a friend? If so, it may suggest they are comfortable and familiar with this behaviour and may use others to provide them with alibis as a return of favour.

When gathering information from an alibi provider you must take care not to let them know that you are on to them, which will be extremely difficult. So a better strategy is to go to their partner.

Alibi providers who are cheats themselves often tell their partners all about their cheating friend and express their disapproval so as to shift attention away from their own questionable behaviour. For this reason the alibi provider's partner is a soft target for information and may even feel pity for your situation.

Telephone the alibi provider's home when you know both he and your partner are not there. Speak to their partner and pretend that your partner claimed they were going to their house. See how they react. Do they flatly deny any knowledge of the arrangement or do they start to panic and make excuses?

Write down all that is said but do not question your partner at this point as to their whereabouts. If your partner starts to use someone or something new as an alibi soon after, you may well have touched on something. Should your partner mention the incident, tell him that you thought he'd told you that he was going to see the alibi partner.

Has your partner recently made new contact with an old school friend or made some new friends?

If so, they won't necessarily introduce you to them straight away. But if they make continued excuses not to do so they may be hiding something and you would be wise to be suspicious.

The following story represents the ultimate in the use of a friend as an alibi. In fact Veronique used her willing twin sister, Francine. Their story may shock some of you!

Veronique and Francine (22) came to England to study for one year as part of the English/French degrees they were both taking in Paris. Their placements were at a top London University.

Veronique and Francine are stunning young women and extremely confident so it was no surprise that they attracted male attention as soon as they arrived. Their rather liberal views on sexuality did nothing to dissuade their various suitors...

Francine: 'I consider sex an activity to be enjoyed the same as football or art. It is there for our pleasure, not for our shame. We all need to free ourselves and learn that if it's enjoyable and, if consent is granted by everyone involved, then it is acceptable.'

The two of them had various flings and one night stands within the first few weeks, often playing tricks on men who didn't realise they were identical twins. Within six weeks Veronique had started seeing two men on a regular basis – Steve (23), a barman in the Stu-dent's Union bar and Bob (43), one of her lecturers. Francine continued to enjoy regular one night stands.

Veronique soon found it difficult juggling the two relationships. She also found she was getting more and more emotionally involved with Bob and less interested in Steve.

Veronique: 'I had never really felt strong emotion towards one man before. Men were there to help me express my sexuality – nothing more. With Bob I suddenly felt different. Maybe it was because he was older, or because he was married, I don't know. I didn't even really want sex with him, not all the time. I wanted to spend time with him, talk to him, buy presents for him. These feelings were all very new to me and I didn't really like it because I had no sense of control.'

Veronique wanted to finish the relationship with Steve but Bob told her not to. He was attracted to her 'liberal' lifestyle and was excited by the idea of being a 'sex object' himself. Bob told Veronique that if she finished with Steve he would no longer have this image of her. Feeling trapped, Veronique agreed to continue with Steve.

Veronique: 'When I had been with Steve, Bob would ask me about it. He wanted all the details. He liked to see me the same day saying it turned him on to think of me having sex with two men within hours of each other. I felt I couldn't object because it would have shattered his image of me.'

So, instead of finishing with Steve, Veronique started to send Francine to meet him in her place – at first only occasionally and then more and more often. Francine was the perfect alibi provider. Not only did she cover the periods when her sister should have been with Steve but she also gave Veronique total freedom to be with Bob whenever she wanted.

Francine acted the part of the loyal girlfriend to perfection, even in the bedroom. She spent plenty of time researching Veronique and Steve's relationship so as to avoid being caught out. She found it fun, at first!

As time went by Veronique became more and more besotted with Bob and Francine became strongly attached to Steve until she found herself feeling extremely jealous when Veronique did spend time with him.

Francine eventually decided that she wanted to see Steve on a 'normal' footing and to tell him and Veronique how she felt.

Veronique put up no objection. She was only interested in Bob and had become so obsessed with him that she had threatened to tell his wife about the affair. However the sisters agreed that they had to keep Veronique's separation from Steve a secret from Bob.

Steve, it transpired, had already discovered the truth. He had become suspicious early on when 'Veronique' sometimes looked at him blankly when he spoke of things they had done together. (Obviously Francine's research had not been thorough enough!). He also found that sex with 'Veronique' would be very different on some nights.

The penny finally dropped after an incident involving Veronique and Bob. When Veronique had threatened to tell Bob's wife of their affair, Bob went crazy and struck Veronique across the face, cutting her lip. Veronique was still visiting Steve occasionally for Bob's sake and Steve obviously questioned her about the cut on a Monday night. But it had miraculously disappeared by Wednesday when Francine took Veronique's place for a trip to the cinema with Steve! Steve had been keeping a record of his 'girlfriend's' strange behaviour for several weeks and this was the final piece of evidence he needed.

Steve confronted 'Veronique' that evening. He told her he had kept a log and that he had found many inconsistencies and contradictions in the stories he had been told by both Veronique and Francine. Francine immediately confessed.

Steve became very angry and told Francine the relationship was over. He felt he had become close to the girl he had been seeing and now didn't know who it was he was supposed to have these feelings for.

Although Francine managed to stop Veronique from shopping Bob to his wife, Bob refused to see her anymore. Before the twins left for Paris at the end of the academic year they visited Bob's office one last time. They poured a litre bottle of mineral water into Bob's computer and super glue into his filing cabinet.

Partial Truth Alibi

Many cheats evade detection because they use alibis
which contain an element of truth. If your partner enjoys
a hobby or sport which calls for time away from home,
he may have the perfect alibi for meeting his mistress
or going out in search of one night stands.

Tim and Sophie had been living together for two
years, although their interests were very different.
Sophie was into Eastern philosophy whilst Tim loved
to go out and party.

Sophie belonged to a yoga club. The fact that
she idolised her teacher, Bret, had not escaped Tim's
attention. One summer Sophie announced that the
club would be making a pilgrimage to Calcutta for
three weeks. Tim didn't mind her going but told her
what he thought about her relationship with Bret.
To Tim's relief, Sophie said that Bret would not be
going to India.

A month before Sophie was due to leave, Tim
made a doctor's appointment for her so that she
could have all the injections which were a prerequi-
site for any visit to India. Sophie thanked him for his

concern but said that she had 'detoxified' herself by using natural herbs and activating a 'source of inner healing'. When Tim advised her to avoid drinking water that wasn't bottled he met with the same response.

Tim kissed Sophie goodbye at Heathrow airport and she boarded her plane. But three days later he was back at the airport. He had been told that Sophie was arriving home on the Air Ambulance, desperately ill.

Tim was allowed to go out onto the tarmac to meet her. The door opened and she was brought down the steps on a stretcher, with a drip attached to her arm. Tim was filled with love and concern. But then another stretcher emerged from the door of the plane carrying a patient similarly afflicted. It was Bret! His herbs and inner healing had apparently failed him too.

It emerged that Tim's suspicions about Sophie and Bret had been justified. The yoga club trip to India was genuine, but it had allowed Sophie to enjoy her new affair with Bret unhindered.

After three weeks in hospital she returned home red faced and full of apologies. Tim had been thinking the whole thing through and decided that Sophie was not the woman for him. He left her and she duly got together with Bret.

It can be difficult to detect whether your partner is only telling part of the truth because they will have access to tangible proof of their whereabouts and spending. However, you should focus in on these to see how much water they hold.

Let's look at a hypothetical situation. Your partner goes fishing regularly with his brother. Or rather, he did that every Sunday for the last three years up until the last six months when he met up with a lover instead.

You have suspicions and you decide to check out the other people mentioned in the alibi. Ring the brother's house on the Sunday and talk to their partner, if they have one. (You can invent a perfectly good reason for calling.) If you find yourself speaking to the brother himself he will be off guard. He will try to offer an explanation for his not being on the trip. Don't ask any questions about your partner – you have already found what you were looking for!

Write down all that is said but do not confront your partner until he has given you his version of events. If he doesn't offer an explanation as soon as he returns, his brother has probably not been able to warn him. He will probably end up talking about the weekend in a matter-of-fact way giving details of what he did with his brother. Record what he says but do not push him any further. Give him enough rope with which to hang himself. Later he will find out for himself that you called his brother's home. He will then try to back pedal on his story: a huge clue!

Check your partner's bank and credit card statements to determine the amount of money he is spending on his Sunday outings. If he is meeting his lover, the chances are that it will be high.

And look at the clothes he is wearing. Are they smart or new? Is he cleaner than usual? Does he wear aftershave? All of this for fishing? You may think not.

Sarah and Nick had been married for eight years. Sarah is a dentist and Nick works as a broker in the City. He was a keen sailor and would spend most weekends on a hired yacht. Sarah shared his pastime in the early days but never with the same enthusiasm as her husband. She also had two children to care for, which took up most of her weekends. So Nick would sail while his wife spent time with her children.

Sarah would often book the yacht for Nick and his friends and knew all the facts about the marina, booking procedures, tariffs and so forth.

One Thursday evening, she was sitting in her kitchen with Nick when the phone rang. Sarah answered it and had a conversation with Nick's friend Jack. He was planning yet another sailing trip and wanted Nick to come along.

Sarah handed over the phone and thought nothing more about it. On Friday night Nick left for the marina where he planned to stay so that the sailing party could get an early start the following morning.

On Saturday Sarah went to buy some clothes for her son and found she needed some petrol for her car. As she drove into the service station she saw Jack pulling out of the car wash facility. Sarah didn't think too much of this because she assumed that something had come up at home for him which had caused him to cancel at the last moment.

Nick came home on Sunday night full of beans and, unprompted, began telling Sarah about his weekend with Jack and the guys on the boat. Sarah had no doubt that she had seen Jack, so she found this confusing. However she didn't confront Nick straight away but asked questions about Jack and the trip that could have no ambiguous answers.

She asked specifically about an ankle injury that had put Jack out of sailing some six months before. Jack's ankle was fine, said Nick, and it hadn't affected his performance on the boat that weekend. Then Sarah asked him whether Jack's partner, Marie, resented the fact that he spent so much time sailing with Nick and two other male friends. Nick said: 'No, not at all. In fact Marie was there on Saturday morning to see us all off'.

By this point, Sarah knew that something was not right but she didn't know what it was. Was Nick having

an affair? Was he providing an alibi for an unfaithful
Jack? Was it something other than infidelity? She
began investigating Nick's 'sailing' weekends. She
kept a record of his spending habits during the trips,
called the marina to see what time he had arrived
and left and (discreetly) asked the marina staff who
was on the yacht with him.

The marina staff told her that there were usually four people on board. That tallied with Nick's
story. What didn't tally however, was that two of
the four were women! On other occasions Sarah
was informed that there were four men on the sailing trip but that Nick was not one of them, even
though he had left home, as usual, with all of his
sailing equipment and clothing.

One Sunday afternoon Sarah waited for Nick at
the marina clubhouse when he sailed in from yet
another trip. She watched as the boat was moored and
Nick disembarked, helping a young lady to the jetty.
She saw Nick give the mystery woman an unambiguous kiss as they walked arm in arm along the jetty.
She couldn't control herself any longer and confronted Nick. He was speechless. He couldn't
believe that he had been caught and asked Sarah
to forgive him. She didn't!

Creating an Alibi Involving You

Earlier I mentioned that aggressive behaviour is an active signal that your partner may be having an affair. Your partner may use this behaviour as a means of provoking an argument. Does your partner end these rows by storming out of the house, only to return later or the following day, full of apologies?

This could be a ploy to get out of the house without having to make an excuse. The last thing you would suspect from a partner in this situation is infidelity.

Unwittingly you may be aiding your partner's infidelity by entering into the procured row and allowing them to 'storm out'. This is not your fault and you should record when it happens.

You can actually steer the procedure so as to gather clues. Believe it or not, the rows may take place at the same time every week or under predictable circumstances. If you feel you have a good idea when the next incident will occur, perform the following steps:

Buy a voice-activated tape recorder or a normal tape recorder (as long as you can hide it) that can achieve at least 30 minutes of taping time. Before the row, place the tape recorder where you will be able to press 'record' discreetly later on. If your telephone has a re-dial button call the speaking clock or any other recorded announcement (I will explain this later), then go to the car and lodge a matchstick in the upper socket of the passenger seatbelt. Do this by pulling the seatbelt about an inch out of its socket and then letting the belt pull itself and the matchstick back into the socket. This will not harm the seatbelt or lessen its effectiveness if there is an accident.

Take a reading of the car mileage, return to the house and wait!

As the incident nears the point at which your partner storms out, have an excuse ready to leave the house for a couple of minutes making sure you turn the tape recorder onto 'record' before you leave. Tell your partner how long you are going to be.

When you return, your partner will either pick up the row where you left off, or they will already have left. When the coast is clear, use the re-dial button on the telephone. Should you hear the speaking clock (or whatever other recorded announcement you dialled) then you will know that your partner has not used the telephone. If you hear a ringing tone, however, your partner has made a call in your absence. Have they called their lover?

Put the receiver down, stop the tape recorder, rewind it and listen to what has been recorded. If your partner called a friend you will probably recognise their name. If the recording does not yield information or doesn't make sense, press the re-dial button again. If a stranger answers try to find out who they are and pretend you dialled a wrong number. If you have dialled a company number, you will hear its name spoken by the telephonist. Your partner may have called their lover at work, so keep a note of the firm's name and mailing address. The reason you might need both tape recording and re-dial button strategies at once is to determine who exactly was on the other end of the phone and to note as many details as possible.

When your partner returns from their jaunt, do not mention the telephone call. Go to the car, check the mileage and look to see if the matchstick is still in place in the seat-belt holder. If someone has used the seat-belt the matchstick will have been dislodged. Look around the car for any other clues, like car-parking tickets. See if it bears any times, dates or locations.

If your detection work has uncovered unpleasant truths it may be impossible for you to hide your feelings. Try to remain calm as once you have 'kissed and made up', you can gently quiz your partner as to their movements while they were away. They will readily offer their prepared 'story'. But does it tie in with the clues you found from the car and the evidence on the tape recorder? How far did they go? Did they meet up with anyone? Give anyone a lift (remember the matchstick!)? Listen to the tape again. List all the evidence given here as well as the evidence uncovered from your car search. And *wait*!

Your Partner Wants You to Go Out

'It's ages since you had a good night out with the girls.'

'Don't worry about me. Go out and have a good time.'

Has your partner begun to show an unhealthy interest in getting you out of the house, perhaps by showing
false concern for you? Sickening as it may sound, many
cheats bring their lover into your home. Perhaps 'getting
out' is becoming tiresome or difficult. Or your cheating
partner and their lover find it erotic to bring their affair
into the 'marital' home and bed.

When did you leave and when did you return? What
did your partner say they were doing whilst you were out?
If they rented a video, ask them about it and find out from
your video store the last tape rented on your card. Did they
watch television? If so, what did they watch? Ask them and
check the television guide.

Your suspicion may lead you to return home unex-
pectedly and catch your partner in the act. Remember
you may witness a scene which you cannot cope with.
Alternatively you may alert your partner's suspicions
which will make it harder to collect further evidence.
If they are innocent you may upset your faithful partner by showing such obvious mistrust.

Lenny had lived with his girlfriend Kelly for two years. Lenny also had a lover, Janine.

One night Kelly was away visiting her sister who had just had a baby. Lenny took the opportunity to sneak Janine into their flat for an evening of passion. Janine left early the next morning and Lenny thought he had covered his tracks perfectly.

On returning from her trip, however, Kelly noticed a few things amiss. Lenny was a health fanatic and would not normally allow people to smoke in the flat. But the place smelt of cigarettes. Second, the flat was spotless. But Lenny never did the cleaning. Third, the bed clothes had been washed. But Lenny had never used the washing machine before. Kelly also found two wine glasses in the dishwasher and, upon further investigation, a wine bottle in the bin.

Kelly confronted Lenny with her suspicions. He claimed he had been on his own all evening and that had tidied up because he felt he had not been pulling his weight around the flat. He claimed both the wine glasses were his.

This wasn't conclusive evidence but it put Kelly on Lenny's track. Over the next few weeks Kelly managed to gather enough hard evidence to trap him into a confession.

The Guilt Trip Alibi

'I was going to go out with the lads but I'm not sure if I want to. After all we said we'd have a look through the holiday brochures.'

'But I don't like to leave you at weekends. It's the only time we really get together, isn't it?'

Does your partner ever express a desire to go out or go away somewhere only to decide against the idea at the last moment because they are feeling tired or depressed or 'not in the mood'?

What is your reaction? Do you ignore them? Do you console them? Or do you, like most partners, actively encourage them to go out: 'Once you get there you'll feel much better'? With your encouragement your partner, apparently grudgingly, drags themselves out.

This could be the 'double bluff' again! You could actually be helping your partner to see their lover. They know how you will respond but want you to think they would rather stay in. They get to go out whilst at the same time assuring themselves that you are not suspicious.

If this happens again, don't encourage them to go out. If they are genuine they will not mention the subject again and will happily settle in front of the television. But if they seem restless and keep on about whether or not to go, you have managed to call their bluff.

Ignore their comments but do observe their behaviour. Do they start pacing around, trying to find a way to get to the phone discreetly? If they become annoyed and irritated with you over something minor then they are probably angry at you for not playing ball. This may lead them to try to cause a row and storm out as I have already described. Before they go, try to ask them about the night out they'd planned. Write it all down.

I conclude this chapter with an extraordinary true-life story which I have quoted at some length because it is so remarkable. Frank had created a situation in which he needed to provide high-quality alibis to two different individuals. For no less than 12 years he managed this, but when it came, his fall from grace was spectacular.

———

Frank was the MD of a computer company. He had a £350,000 house in central London, a top-of-the-range Mercedes, and had been married to Jill for 12 years. They had four children. Frank was frequently away from home on business.

But Frank also had a council house several hours' drive north, in Leeds, a 10 year-old bottom-of-the-range car and had been married to Sandy for 14 years. They had three children. Sandy thought Frank was a struggling freelance travelling salesman. Again, this called for periods away from home.

Frank would spend two weeks at a time with each wife. In London he would live the high life, wearing fancy clothes, eating in expensive restaurants and going on exotic holidays. In Leeds he would dress in off-the-peg clothes, eat takeaway food and take holidays in the British seaside resort Blackpool.

Christmas and Easter were always a problem for Frank as he was expected to be in two places at the same time. Also the birthday of one of his children in London fell on the same date as the birthday of another of his children in Leeds.

Yet he was discovered by accident!

Sandy: 'Frank had played the poor salesman very convincingly with me. My dad used to give him money to tide him over. Although he was great with the kids I will never forgive him for that. One day I bought Sammy, our eight-year-old son, a computer magazine. An hour afterwards he came running in saying that dad was in the magazine and that he was famous. There in full colour was a picture of Frank and an article about his success in the computer industry. Frank was wearing an expensive suit and was apparently sitting at his desk in his London office. The article said he lived in London with his wife and four kids. The only thing that was the same was his name. I'm an asthmatic and immediately had an attack.

'Obviously the magazine article didn't give
details of Frank's London address so I did a little
detective work on the phone. I called his company
and got the address of his business and the area
in which he lived. I gave the telephonist enough
information to convince her to tell me which street
Frank lived on in London. I told her I wanted to
send him a gift from my fictitious company. Then
I called directory enquiries for his number.

'It was Thursday and Frank was due to come
home that weekend. I told my mum and dad and
they went mad. Our solicitor told us to be careful
and that it was a matter for the police. I was too
scared to call Frank's number but I was also becoming more and more angry. When he turned up as
usual on Friday night I couldn't control myself. I
called him a callous b*****d and tried to kick him.
I told him I was on to him and that I was going to
contact his other wife and tell the police. Suddenly
this man who had been kind and calm for years
became aggressive and intimidating. He slapped me
and threatened to kill me and take my children
back to Jordan. In that one evening I realised that
I was married to a stranger who had been stringing
me along for years.

'Before he left he told me – chillingly – to be
'very careful'. The next morning Frank called me
and threatened me again. He told me how easy it
would be to take the boys whenever he felt like it.

In the next 10 days Frank started to terrorise me. He would call me in the middle of the night and tell me he was coming to kill me and that I should lock the doors. He sent me dog's excrement through the post. My mother kept on at me to go to the police. Then I received another call from Frank – this time surprisingly friendly. He told me he was going back to Jordan and would send money for the boys if I kept quiet about the situation. Suddenly I knew how scared he actually was.

'A few days after Frank called, a strange man tried to pick up the children from school. My mother told me that if I didn't go to the police, she would. I decided to call the 'other woman'. Jill answered and I was amazed how nice she was. We agreed to meet in a restaurant in London. She had no idea what I was going to tell her and I told her not to let Frank know she was meeting me.'

Jill: 'I thought that Sandy was Frank's mistress! I blamed myself for there being a problem within the relationship that had driven him to have an affair. When we met, Sandy and I didn't exchange any form of greeting. We just sat down and Sandy began to talk. I remember feeling as if I was watching something on television. Waves of panic washed over me as the truth sank in. Eventually we both broke down in tears.'

Sandy: 'I had prepared myself for the meeting but not for getting so upset! The meeting was actually much more difficult than the threats and worry of the previous week. I felt like I was in the headmaster's office telling him about some mischief I'd been in. My voice was quivering and my whole body was shaking. I didn't know how Jill would respond.

'I had become used to a situation which was new to Jill. When we broke down together I felt relieved. Our friendship was bonded in that moment.'

Over the course of their talk, many mysterious incidents in both Jill and Sandy's past with Frank now became clear.

Jill: 'When he went away to conferences and various business trips I couldn't contact him as he would be too busy to be distracted by telephone calls. I did find it strange that he would always leave his mobile phone behind, however. I know now he was very sly. For example, he solved the problem of spending his birthday with his 'wife' by having two birthdays!'

Sandy: 'Each Christmas he caused a row either at Jill's or mine on Christmas Eve and stormed out. When he returned on Boxing Day or New Year's Eve, I was so worried about him that I didn't question where he had been. He would say that he had stayed with his cousins. None of them could speak English so I never called him there.'

Not only did they understand the facts of their shared history, they shared many of the same emotional responses to the situation.

Jill: 'You were the only person in the world who understood how I felt, not least because we thought we knew the same man intimately.'

Sandy: 'I thought she might think I was some jealous, vengeful, jilted mistress trying to twist the knife. But, as well as telling her about Frank's double life, I let her know how I was feeling deep down. Bizarre as the situation was I hadn't had another woman to discuss it with, apart from my mum, because I felt so ashamed of myself.'

Jill: 'Frank became a stranger in my eyes and I dreaded going home to him. He hadn't been away for several weeks and I had been enjoying having him home. The situation reminded me of that old 'B' movie I Married a Monster from Outer Space but this was reality and I was terrified. When I walked in Frank was reading the paper and asked where I had been. He guessed the truth by the look in my eyes. I made a cup of tea and then, all of a sudden, started to smash everything! Frank and the children came running into the kitchen and I stopped when I saw how it was scaring the children.

'Frank took the children into their playroom and told them not to come out. He came back and asked me what the problem was and tried to cuddle me. I pushed him off and swore at him. His caring look turned into an angry stare. Frank had hit me a few times in the past and I was scared, but I still told him that I knew about Sandy and demanded an explanation. He laughed and said that the woman was mad and that he had no knowledge of her.

'For a wonderful moment I believed him. When I approached him again, this time in the bedroom, he denied it once more and actually tried to entice me into bed. I found this blatant attempt to distract me quite disgusting. When I declined his advances he became violent, pushing me against the door and becoming verbally abusive.

'I slept in another room that night. The next morning he informed me he was going back to Jordan and was taking the children to visit their grandparents. I remembered the threats that he'd given Sandy about kidnapping her children and alarm bells started ringing in my head.

'I gave him some excuse about visiting my mother that day and left with all the children in tow. Frank was already on the telephone booking the flight for him and the children for the following week. I called Sandy from my mother's and she told me to stay away from Frank as she thought he was serious about taking the children.'

Sandy: 'Later the same day Frank called me and started abusing me. He claimed I had ruined his life and said some day he would 'pay' me back. It was at that point that my brothers got involved. They went crazy when they heard what was going on and drove to London to 'see' Frank. By the time they called at Jill's home in London Frank had fled the country. He hadn't any money to speak of here in Leeds but he emptied his London account.'

Jill: 'Yes, but not before I withdrew a substantial sum for the children's upkeep. He has also tried to sell the house but I cannot speak about that at the moment. Suffice to say that we are waiting for a substantial settlement in the not-too-distant future.

'When Frank left he continued to send letters threatening to take all seven children to Jordan. This was another reason to stay in contact with Sandy. Eventually we decided to get together and pool our resources.'

Sandy: 'We have decided to wait until the children are a little older before we tell them the truth. They still miss their father which can be upsetting for us when we know what an animal he really is. Both of the older boys are beginning to ask questions we will have to answer soon.

Our advice to anybody who finds themselves in a position similar to ours is get out of there fast! Don't let anyone waste your time or treat you like a piece of property.'

Jill: 'Yes, and don't let anyone victimise or threaten you in any way. There is always an alternative, no matter how trapped you feel.'

Sandy and Jill now share a house – and a bed – together. They became extremely close during their shared trauma and realised they could never let another man get close to them again.

Sandy: 'It's a truly loving relationship. One thing we can thank Frank for is that all the children are related to one another. We have a ready-made family within a lesbian relationship.'

Chapter 4

Hard Evidence

By now you have probably decided for yourself whether or not your partner is being unfaithful to you. But do you have enough evidence with which to confront them? Just because you have disproved their alibi there may still be some good reason why they are lying. No case is really complete without some hard evidence and, in this chapter, I will tell you how to get it.

Bank Account Evidence

It's quite unnerving to consider how our financial behaviour can cast light upon our lifestyle and movements. It makes us a target for highly specialised marketing and also offers high-quality evidence to the police if we break the law. Bank statements can give you some excellent hard evidence of your partner's infidelity. And remember, what doesn't appear on a person's financial statement can be as significant as what does.

Like all records of this kind, bank account details vary substantially from bank to bank and from country to country. You will, however usually be given the dates upon which cheques have been presented, their individual numbers and the amount in each case. Cross-refer with the cheque stubs to find the actual date the cheque was written. If the stub has been left blank, look at the stubs immediately before and after it. Record the dates because at least then you will know the approximate dates when the suspect cheque was written. A blank cheque stub is a possible indicator in itself – particularly if your partner is usually careful about their finances.

Refer back to all the records that you have been keeping over the past weeks.

Armed with your list of suspect incidents, alibis, names, places and times, look at your partner's next bank account statement. You will probably see immediately whether everything is as it should be.

Are there unexplained hotel or restaurant payments that seem mysteriously to contradict an alibi? Are there purchases from unusual stores?

In an effort to avoid detection, some unfaithful partners use cash. However, when a cash withdrawal is made, the bank statement not only gives information about the amount withdrawn but the date of withdrawal and the bank location.

Why is there evidence of a regular withdrawal at a certain point in the week or month? Why did your partner take money out of a cashpoint in Birmingham when they said they were in Bristol that day? Why didn't they withdraw much cash on those two days when they were supposed to be away on a stag/hen weekend? Why did they spend money in that particular store? Why does one location keep cropping up? Why did they withdraw one hundred pounds on the night when they were having dinner round at their mum's? Remember to look for what is *not* there as well as checking the information that is provided.

———

Debbie's partner Jason went away for three nights one November, claiming he would be undertaking training at his firm's office in a British south coast town. He mentioned that he would be paying for the trip and all the other expenses – such as meals out with clients – with his debit card. He would claim the money back from the company after the trip.the matter. One morning his bank statement arrived. He opened it but left it unread on the kitchen table. Debbie picked it up innocently, looking for clues as to the nature of her Christmas present from him. Instead she noticed something strange.

There were payments for a hotel bill and other goods purchased in a British west coast holiday resort dating back, she worked out, to the three days he was supposed to be on his south coast business trip. No payments had been made in that area.

Debbie noticed this purely by accident. Had she suspected her partner's infidelity previously and kept records of his supposed trips away she would have been able to use this tactic to catch him out sooner. She later discovered that this had not been his first bogus business trip away.

Jason was completely unprepared when he was confronted with this hard evidence. He realised he was caught and admitted to the truth.

———————

Brian had suspected his wife Joanne of having an affair for some time when he noticed something strange on their joint account statement.

Joanne would use her Visa card to pay for the week's shopping and other expenses, rarely using the cashpoint facility. Several entries on the bank statement, however, showed that Joanne was using a cashpoint more often than normal and it was not at their local branch.

He telephoned his bank and discovered the mystery branch was some twenty miles out of town. He started to suspect that his wife was keeping something from him.

Brian then noticed that she was also doing her shopping in the same location, as the branch code of the supermarket showed in the Visa entries. All this evidence led Brian to employ other techniques outlined in this guide. Eventually he confronted his wife with so much evidence that Joanne had no choice but to admit her infidelity. She had in fact been meeting her lover in the afternoon and using a bank and a supermarket near his home.

Where Did All that Cash Go?

If your partner is using cash to finance their infidelity, the sums will be considerable. So look at the amounts withdrawn and ask yourself where they have gone. A meal, after-dinner drinks, dancing and a night in a hotel will add up to a lot of money in anybody's terms. Record the incident because you will be asking your partner for justification later.

———————

Gary (33) was a service engineer earning good wages. He and his wife Sheila (29) had a large mortgage which consumed most of their joint income. Until he met his wife, Gary was a virgin. He had been unable to get a girlfriend and had always felt robbed of the teenage sexual exploits his friends would brag about.

Gary: 'It all began one night as I came home from the pub after a snooker tournament. I'd taken a short-cut and found myself walking through the town's red light district, though I didn't know it at the time.

'All of a sudden this lovely girl dressed in a tight mini-skirt and a revealing top stepped out of a door-way and asked me if I was 'business'. I didn't have a clue what this meant. I suppose I was a little naive but I was also turned on by her. She told me that I was a good looking fella and that she found me sexy. It was a load of old nonsense I know, but I was never a great success with girls and had never had sex with another woman. I paid her and she gave me oral sex in an alley.

'When I got home I felt great! After that I couldn't stop myself. I'd go down to the red light area as often as possible and have full sex with at least four girls a week. I decided to sleep with every prostitute in the area. They were black, Chinese, blonde, brunette, even a French student studying here in England.

'For the first time in my life I was being promiscuous and I gloried in it! The problem was that I had started to spend money that Sheila and I needed for the mortgage. My wife started checking the bank account every week. She thought I was gambling the money away. She finally put two and two together when she realised that I would draw the money out on my way home from work or after I had been to the pub. She knew that I didn't have time to draw the money out on the way to work as the bank was a distance from my place of work.

'I began to default on the mortgage but I couldn't stop spending money on the girls.'

Gary found himself cruising the red light district even when he hadn't the money to buy sex. Just looking gave him a thrill. One night he was stopped by the police for kerb crawling and for the first time he saw the implications of his actions.

The fact that he didn't have any money cut no ice with the police officers. When Gary was able to say where he had been and where he was going, however, they let him go.

Gary was frightened by the experience and decided to give up this 'hobby'. During the next three weeks his wife spoke to him about Gamblers Anonymous because she thought their money was going on the horses.

Eventually, however, the draw to have sex was so powerful that Gary couldn't stop himself going to the

red light district. Five minutes after he started cruising the area, he was stopped again.

'The day I was stopped by the police for the
second time, I was terrified. It was the same offi-
cer who'd heard my cock and bull story the last
time. This time he collared me and took me down
to the police station. I was told to report to the
local court the following Monday to answer alle-
gations of kerb crawling. We had a funeral to
attend that day so the police did me a big favour
by changing the date.

'However, that was also my undoing because
a summons was sent to my home address. My wife
found it and opened it straight away. As I came down
the stairs she started to shout and cry. I felt very
small and was completely embarrassed by the whole
affair. My wife told me she had been on to me for a
long time because of the cash withdrawals and that
the summons only proved her suspicions.

'I admitted all and, to her credit, my wife came
with me to the court. I was fined and ordered to stay
away from the red light district. We lost the house as
a result of my behaviour and my wife has left me. I'm
afraid I have taken to the bottle but I'm doing something about that as we speak.'

Gary has recently started going to AA and is
trying to build his life again. He is fighting the
temptation to visit prostitutes but admits to having

'moments of weakness'. He hopes to get back together
with his wife one day.

Credit Cards

Credit cards are frequently used to pay for indiscretions, and cheats may take little notice of the evidence
they will yield. They are quick and easy and are useful
when the subject has not got enough money in their
account to pay for their philandering. Money worries
take second place to the thrill of the chase. Has your
partner recently started using the credit card to its
limit? Do you know why?

Credit card statements give as much information
as a bank account statement. They show the name of
the recipient – be it a shop, restaurant, night club or
hotel – and the date on which the transaction took
place. Also, it is possible to withdraw cash with a credit
card. Given that this is an expensive way of obtaining
money, an individual requires a very good story with
which to justify it. Again you can expect to see the date
of the withdrawal and where the money was taken from
(usually in the form of an abbreviated bank location
and specific code for the particular bank in question).

Telephone Bills

The amount of information that appears on telephone bills varies wildly. At best you can expect a precise record of the date, time and length of all calls, but some companies will only detail the more expensive calls.

Are your telephone bills unusually large? Do unfamiliar numbers regularly appear? Were these calls made when you were not at home? A record of your own movements in the preceding weeks will help you determine the answer.

Put the suspect numbers, dates and times into your dossier. I will describe telephone entrapment in Chapter Five.

Car Checking

A car gives cheats the freedom to conduct their affair away from their home territory and reduces the risk of being spotted by those who know them. It also goes without saying that it offers a convenient (if cramped) venue for illicit liaisons.

During the early days of an affair your partner will probably be extremely careful not to leave any incriminating evidence in the car. However, as he becomes more

comfortable with the situation, he will invariably become
less vigilant. We all regard a car as personal space, particularly if it is our own and not shared with our partner.
If you suspect your partner of using the car for a rendezvous, take the following steps:

1) Record the mileage.

2) Search the glove compartment, door pockets and
   ashtrays.

3) Scan the inside of the car for marks.

4) Search the inside of the car, remembering to look
   down the sides of seats.

5) Look in the boot.

6) Check the outside of the car.

We will cover each of these checks in turn.

1. Record the Mileage

Armed with car mileage data you can determine the
average distance your partner covers driving to work,
their leisure pursuit and other regular locations. Don't

forget to calculate it on a round-trip basis. To verify the mileage you can either drive the routes yourself, take a taxi or get a friend to drive you. Mileage information will never be precise as we all use different routes, give people lifts home and the like.

Once you have this data you can 'measure' the validity of your partner's alibis.

Wendy (24) had been married to Clive (24) for two years. They had no children and rented an apartment just outside London. Clive was an office manager. He wasn't really a drinking man but, all of a sudden, began going for a 'quick drink' after work. He told Wendy that his companion was a guy he was working with and that he enjoyed it – it helped him to unwind.

Wendy thought this so out of character for Clive that she became suspicious. It was impossible to follow Clive to verify his story because she couldn't drive. After some thought however Wendy came up with an ingenious strategy. Every morning when she picked up the bottles of milk from her doorstep she also recorded the mileage on Clive's car.

On the days Clive didn't go for a drink after work the round trip was about 24 miles from home to

work and back again. On the evenings when he did go
out the mileage climbed to 58 miles. Then Wendy asked
Clive about the location of the bar and whether he gave
anyone a lift home afterwards. Clive told her that the
bar was en route from work and that the other guys
from work had their own transport.

Wendy began looking through Clive's pockets
when he was out. She found cash withdrawal slips
from the bank with the same date as one of his
drinking trips. He had withdrawn more money than
he would customarily need for a whole week, let
alone for a 'quick drink'.

By cross-referencing the dates on Clive's bank
statements with the mileage records, Wendy began to
see a pattern emerge. Clive would spend large sums
of money on each of the nights that the mileage hit
that suspect 58–60 miles. Armed with this information Wendy called a private detective. He required
just one day to find the truth because Wendy had
gathered all the necessary evidence for him. He followed Clive from work and watched as he called
Wendy to tell her that he was going for a drink. That
he did but it was with a woman who turned out to be
someone who worked in the same building as Clive.

After the drink Clive drove the woman to a
hotel where they had a meal and then disappeared
into one of the rooms for an hour or so. When they
emerged, Clive took the mystery woman home

(in the opposite direction to his own home) and the reason for the discrepancy in the car mileage became apparent. With several pictures taken by the private investigator as hard evidence and a large amount of substantial (yet circumstantial) evidence of her own, Wendy confronted Clive.

He went into denial mode. He told Wendy that the investigator had followed the wrong man, that there was nothing between him and any girl from work and that she shouldn't be so mistrusting of him. For a brief moment Wendy believed him even though the truth was staring her in the face. Wendy believes that this was because she desperately wanted to be wrong.

Eventually Wendy did get a confession out of Clive but was so traumatised by the way Clive violently denied his infidelity that she felt she couldn't trust him again and divorced him soon after. Wendy has since met another partner who works from home!

---

2. Search the Glove Compartment, Door Pockets and Ashtrays

Many unfaithful mates are caught out by their partners when they leave something incriminating in the glove box or door pockets. You may find parking tickets, paid parking stickers or promotional flyers, breath fresheners, combs, hairbrushes, lipsticks, keys, sweet wrappers, tickets for the theatre, cinema or clubs. Every piece of paper tells a story. Record details of all such material.

As a passenger in a car it is easy to distractedly leave keys, wallets and purses in the glove box with the intention of removing them on leaving the vehicle. After a night of wining, dining and excitement however, the contents of the glove box would be the last thing on your mind.

If your partner smokes or chews gum they will use the ashtray to discard the waste. You may feel a little silly sifting through the ashtray but it too can yield important clues. And while combing the car for evidence might seem, on the face of it, demeaning, remember that the goal of your search to find the truth is to put an end to a situation that is potentially much more demeaning (being cheated on by the one you trust!).

Are the cigarette ends the brand your partner smokes? Are they marked with lipstick? Look for fragments of condom wrappers as well as car parking tickets.

Seemingly inconsequential evidence can sometimes be the decisive factor in discovering a cheat.

———————

Paul discovered that his wife, Samantha, had been cheating on him when he discovered a flier in the glove compartment of their car!

Paul used the car every day and knew what was usually in the glove compartment. One day he found a flier advertising a sale at a central London carpet warehouse that had not been there the previous day. The day before Samantha had used the car to visit a friend who supposedly lived outside the London area. As fliers are distributed locally, Paul wondered how this one could have got into his glove compartment.

Paul decided to confront his wife. He chose an all or nothing strategy. When he returned home from work he decided to call Samantha's bluff and told her that he had followed her the previous evening, giving the general area. Then he sat back and waited for her response. After five minutes Samantha began to break down and eventually told all.

She had been out for a night with her lover in London and had taken the flier from the windscreen and put it in the glove box without a second thought.

3. Scan the Inside of the Car for Marks

Check the upholstery, carpets, windows and roof for evidence. The carpets may tell you how many people were in the car, the weather and environment in which the suspect incident took place. Mud or gravel deposits suggest a country environment whereas road stones or glass probably came from a city street.

If your partner has picked someone up from a muddy environment they will probably not have got out of the car. The passenger carpet will therefore be muddy and the driver's carpet clean.

If you can clean the passenger carpet before your partner leaves for their 'meeting' you will be able to see at a glance whether or not someone has been sitting in the passenger seat. In fact – as we will see in the next chapter – it is good to check to make sure the car is clean as often as possible.

———

Marcia and Stuart lived together. Stuart regularly borrowed Marcia's car and, due to his carelessness, it was here that she discovered the clues to his infidelity.

Each time Marcia loaned Stuart the car she noticed strange marks on the passenger carpet. She described these as long, thin scorings in the carpet with puncture marks at either end.

When she quizzed Stuart he would accuse her of being paranoid. He said the marks had been made by his sports bag. Marcia borrowed Stuart's bag and placed the bag on the front passenger carpet as she had seen Stuart do. The marks on the carpet were not the same.

It wasn't until Marcia wore a pair of stiletto shoes to a party that she realised what had actually caused the marks!

When Stuart next borrowed the car, Marcia (with the help of a friend) followed and saw him pick up another woman!

———————————————

Look for strands of hair on the headrests and marks on the seats. Look for foot and handprints on the windows, the windscreen and the roof lining.

4. Search the Inside of the Car

A variety of debris finds its way under the car seats, usually without the knowledge of driver or passenger. You never know what you might find.

Many smaller items can be lost down the back of a car seat – rings, earrings, fragments of condom wrappers and so forth.

Steve (29) had been living with his girlfriend, Jenny (30) for 18 months. Everyone thought them the perfect couple and Steve was considering proposing to Jenny.

One Sunday afternoon Steve was driving home from football practice and noticed a comb sticking out from under the passenger seat of his car. Jenny had borrowed the car the previous evening to go out on a 'girl's night'.

Steve was a little puzzled about the comb because it was a man's – small, flat and black. He knew it wasn't there the day before because he cleaned the car for Jenny's night out. What was a woman doing with a man's comb? Steve knew all the women who were supposed to be out with Jenny and none of them had hairstyles that would have needed a comb like this.

Steve decided to leave the comb under the seat in the hope that Jenny would see it and explain the situation without him having to confront her. As they were going out for a meal that night Steve was sure that she would see the comb jutting out from under the seat. That night however, it was all but invisible in the darkness.

Steve began checking the car on a regular basis whenever Jenny used it on her own. Several times he found cigarette butts in the ashtray when Jenny had claimed to be visiting a friend. Jenny's friend didn't smoke, neither did Jenny. What's more her friend wouldn't have used the passenger seat because Jenny would visit her at her home.

Steve registered the mileage each time too and soon discerned a pattern of unexplained longer journeys. He was soon able to predict when Jenny would next take the car on one of her long trips. Using a car loaned from a friend, he followed her.

Steve was shocked to see Jenny stop at a public toilet. She went in wearing a sweatshirt and jeans with the sports bag she used for her aerobics classes. Five minutes later she re-emerged wearing a very provocative evening dress. She was obviously going somewhere special.

Steve followed the car on to a bar where a well-dressed man met her with open arms. Steve became irrational and confronted them both. He threw some punches at the mystery man who was terrified. The doormen stepped in to stop the fight and Steve was thrown out of the bar shouting threats and abuse at Jenny and the man she was with.

He went home and half an hour later Jenny turned up. She was obviously embarrassed and guilty about the situation and pleaded for forgiveness. Unfortunately, Steve was too angry to respond in a sensible manner and struck her instead. Then he left the house and went to a bar to drown his sorrows. When he returned Jenny was gone. She had taken her clothes and gone to her sister's flat. Two months later Jenny and Steve met up and talked the whole thing through. Jenny has moved back in with Steve but the future isn't clear.

———

5. Look in the Boot

Cheats often have a secret store of clothing into which they change when they meet their lover. This may be kept in a holdall in the boot of the car.

Check the boot. Look in your partner's sports bag for unusual garments. Look for a space in the boot for the bag. Check for labels – such as airline baggage tags –

that may have fallen off the bag. Check the spare tyre compartment too for hidden objects.

6. Check the Outside of the Car

Did your partner's alibi feature a breakdown? Check the tyres and mudflaps for mud or gravel deposits. Search the bodywork for mud. If the car has recently been cleaned, check the headlights for insect deposits.

If a motorway trip does not feature in your partner's alibi how did the insects get there? Your partner must have driven the car somewhere at speed to gather the insect deposits.

Checking Clothes

How many times have you found old telephone numbers, receipts and notes in your own clothes? Many times, I have no doubt. They could give you the last piece of the jigsaw in proving your partner's infidelity. Search jacket pockets for telephone numbers (especially numbers without names), cash withdrawal slips, cinema or theatre tickets, parking stickers and strange notes. It can be helpful to remind yourself why you are doing this: to preserve your dignity in the long term.

Remember to check breast pockets as most people forget about using them. Check trousers too and do not forget the turn-ups!

If there are holes in the pockets check the lining for any evidence that may have slipped through the holes.

You may detect the scent of perfume or aftershave. Identify the brand if you can because you may smell it again in the car or elsewhere later. Look for lipstick on shirts and hair strands on jackets and jumpers.

In the following case study Shirley finds hard evidence of her husband's infidelity in the course of checking his clothes. Dave, the cheat in question, had been exhibiting classic 'passive' signals. And Shirley is herself the classic 'accidental' cheat.

Shirley (22) harboured suspicions that her husband Dave (26) was having an affair. One night Dave's father, Graham (47), went around to their house when Dave was out.

Shirley: 'I was completely besotted with Dave in the early years and we were a real adventurous couple. However, when he began to act strangely I soon became aware of the thin line between love and hate. In the space of two months Dave went from being a

loving and respectful husband to being an emotionless
zombie who would look on me with contempt.

'For no reason that I could see, our sex life became
non-existent and Dave would spend hours in front of
the television doing his best not to make eye contact
with me. He would also go for long drives and spend a
disproportionate amount of time with his friends. At
first I thought he was depressed so I tried to be understanding towards him. In fact he was seeing Tracey all
the time and taking me for an idiot.

'Graham had come to see Dave and, while we
waited for him, we opened a bottle of wine. Then Dave
called to say that something had come up and that he
was staying at his best friend's house – again. At that
point I slammed the phone down and started swearing
and shouting about Dave.

'Graham was very good and calmed me down.
We talked about life, love and marriage and I
remember thinking for a second that I had married
the wrong man. How lucky my mother-in-law was
to have such an understanding man! I was still
looking at Graham purely as my father-in-law,
but I realised I really admired him.

'As the night went on we talked about our
lives, our hopes and our fears and we finished a
second bottle of wine. When Graham decided to
go we were both merry and I showed him to the
front door. It was dark in the hall because the light
in the hall was broken. Graham turned to give me

the usual father-in-law/daughter-in-law peck on the cheek and it just developed into a full blown kiss.

'I was shocked by the situation and could hardly believe it was happening, but neither of us could stop. Eventually we made love right there on the hall floor and, bizarre as it was, I found the whole thing wonderful. I can honestly say that I had no intention of sleeping with Graham but, in the event, I felt released from the stress of Dave and all his goings-on. The next day, however, I was a wreck. The reality of the situation hit me and I realised that I had just slept with the father of my cheating husband.

'I think I started to fall in love with Graham when he rang to apologise for his behaviour and to offer any help I needed. I thought it would be sensible for us to stay away from each other for a while and Graham agreed. When Dave returned he began spouting some nonsense about why he spent the night away from home. I just said 'yeah, yeah' and ignored him. Somehow I felt excited that Dave had been with 'her' without knowing that I had been with his dad. From then on I started to treat Dave the same way he had treated me. He hated it!

'I began to really suspect Dave of being unfaithful when I was doing the weekly wash. I would check all the pockets for money, handkerchiefs and so forth. Then I came across something that shocked me. I remember thinking how weak a storyline this would be in a film. But here I was looking at a receipt signed by my husband for a night in a hotel room with a meal in the restaurant.

'The date on the receipt was 24th June – three days before and the night he had supposedly spent at his best friend's house. One of the entries was for a telephone call made from the room, showing the time it was made. This was when he had phoned me to say that he was staying at his friend's house. I started to search his clothes on a regular basis and found lots of receipts for goods and hotel rooms of which I had no knowledge.

'One thing I found that really upset me was tickets for a well-known zoo and theme park. I realised that Dave was doing the whole romantic bit with somebody else and I began to hate him for it. He was so deceitful. He explained away his behaviour by saying that he needed some time alone and all that rubbish. I don't know why but I was too scared to confront him directly about what I had found. I just kept going, hoping that it would sort itself out sooner or later.

'About a week later the in-laws were due to come for dinner and I was not looking forward to it. Things were awkward for the first half hour or so, and then we began to relax. Dave went into the kitchen to talk with his mum Patricia, leaving me and Graham on our own in the sitting room. Graham got up, walked across the room and kissed me. He took control of the situation and I just melted.

'As he kissed me I could hear Dave and his mum talking in the kitchen – it was really exciting. After that we couldn't keep away from each other. Every time Dave went out I would call Graham and he would come around and we would have great sex together. One day I realised that the great sex had turned into great lovemaking!

'It wasn't all roses, however. I felt tremendous guilt towards Patricia. She had always been good to me and I felt a deep connection with her. Despite my attachment to her I began to see her as an obstacle in the way of me and Graham.

'After six weeks of this bizarre lifestyle, Graham asked me to run off with him! Without a moment's thought I accepted. Even though I knew it would cause a lot of pain within the family I also knew that it was the right thing for me to do.

'I have to admit we were cowards. Instead of facing Dave and his mother with the truth we decided to leave notes and just run off. I am bitterly disgusted with myself for not confronting the situation properly. I cannot ever see a time when we could all be in the same room together without there being a terrible scene.

'I am expecting Graham's baby and we are both very excited about it. Graham treats me as the most special person in his life and, if our history was different, we'd be seen as the perfect couple. I have not

told Dave or Patricia about the baby yet. I suppose I
am reluctant to face them, especially Dave's mum,
the real victim of this story. She's been on tablets
for her nerves ever since it started. Apart from this,
I have no regrets.

'Dave is living with his lover now. I think that it's
worked out pretty well for him. After all, I didn't confront him about her did I? Do you know that the same
night I left a note telling him about me and his dad,
he was going to tell me about the other woman?'

———

Keys

If your partner is involved in a long term affair the chances
are that they will possess a key to the other person's home.

It will be on their key ring along with the keys to your
house and car. After all, you would never guess from a
key that your partner was being unfaithful, would you?

Look on your partner's key ring for keys you cannot
explain and remove the first one!

Keep this key for a number of weeks and one of three
things might happen:

1) Your partner complains that they have lost a key and tells you what it was for. They will probably describe a cupboard at work or a locker at their hobby centre they could not gain access to. Soon after this you 'find' the key...

2) Your partner says nothing and a copy of the key does not appear on the key ring. This probably means that the key was obsolete and your partner has not even noticed that it was missing.

3) Your partner has a copy of the key made and it appears on their key ring soon after, without their mentioning it to you. This is a highly suspect situation and could indicate deceit. After all, if you lost an important key, surely you'd complain to your partner about it?

Once you have acquired several pieces of hard evidence you are well on your way to confronting and catching the cheat. In the next chapter I will tell you how to set up situations or 'traps' which will either give you conclusive evidence of your partner's infidelity or further hard evidence for your dossier.

Chapter 5

Following Your Partner
and Setting Traps

Following Your Partner

It is tempting to decide that capturing your partner with the other man or woman is the only sure method of determining the truth. This is by no means as easy as television detectives make it appear.

It is often difficult logistically and it is certainly difficult psychologically. Consider the following before you try 'tailing' somebody:

- If you are following your partner's car in another car, you are unlikely to be paying enough attention to other cars, pedestrians or animals.

- If you are following an individual on a bus or train you will probably bump into other passengers and cause irritation.

- If you see your partner with another man or woman you will become upset and may act irrationally. You will probably want to leave the scene as soon as possible and will probably be showing the world that you are in distress and therefore vulnerable.

———————

One evening Kerry followed her boyfriend Peter and her brother Greg because she believed they were going out to see some girls. She was angry with her brother as she had always trusted him to keep her best interests at heart.

Kerry: 'Peter and I met about five years ago, when we were both 23. We were cabin crew on the same flight to Vienna, and when we arrived the whole crew decided to have a drink in my room at the hotel. After an hour the others left and then there was only myself and Peter chatting and messing about. We made love and so our relationship began.

'We moved into a flat together and we lived a life rich with good sex and great times. Our friends envied our relationship and would ask us for the secret. My family liked Peter and he got on well with my brother Greg (29).

'I never suspected Peter of having an affair until I found a condom wrapper when I was cleaning out our car. The worst thing was that it was just a corner,

meaning that it had been used. I immediately thought
he had been having sex with another woman.

'I started going through his pockets, studying the
phone bill and so on. There were a lot of calls to my
mum's house and evidence of visits to certain bars but
I didn't consider them suspicious at the time.

'I followed Peter a couple of times with no result.
Eventually, I began to think that the condom was
part of a joke or something. I stopped following him
and dropped the whole thing.

'Peter often went out for a drink with Greg and
I never thought to follow him then. One night,
however, Peter got home at 3.30am and I noticed
something unusual. If I'd been out for the night I
would come home stinking of cigarette smoke,
alcohol and perspiration. Peter was as sweet
smelling as when he left. He smelt of toothpaste,
shower gel and aftershave. How and where could he
have taken a shower after the club? I was furious. It
dawned on me that Peter had been seeing another
woman with the blessing of my brother.

'One Wednesday evening I decided to follow them
when they went to London. As soon as they pulled out
of our drive to go to the station, I ran to our car and
started chasing them. It was a dangerous thing to do
and I narrowly missed hitting a car when I pulled out
of a turning.

'At the station I hid in the doorway of the station
kiosk while they bought their tickets. When the train

arrived in London I had to wait until they were nearly off the platform before I got off the train. This made the people behind me very angry and I was called a few names. As I followed them out I bumped into several more people. Peter was holding Greg's arm and, as they walked towards a club, they put their arms round each other. I thought they were messing around until, as they went in, Greg put his arm round Peter in an intimate way and gave him a little squeeze. They went up the stairs and, just before they disappeared from sight, Peter gave Greg a proper kiss.

'I felt numb and nauseous as though I was going to pass out. It was like being on a film set. I thought I must have been imagining things. I can't remember the walk back to the station. I do remember looking at other couples, thinking how happy they looked and resenting them for it.

'I felt betrayed by Greg, who was always there when I had a problem. The thought of him kissing my boyfriend made me feel sick and gave me a head rush of jealousy as well. I hated Peter and loved him at the same time and for one stupid moment on the train I cried out that it was all my fault. I didn't care if the other passengers heard me.

'I missed my station and had to wait an hour for the train to bring me back just one stop. As I waited, I started imagining what was going on in the club at the same time. I was almost enjoying the jealous rage it put me in.

'The next morning Peter and Greg arrived home around 10.30 in the morning. Peter told me I looked terrible and he was right. I hadn't slept at all and felt terribly stressed. Greg told me to 'stick the kettle on' and I did! I suppose I was in what they call 'denial'. Greg left after drinking his tea and Peter gave me a hug. For some strange reason I really found him attractive and 'needed' to make love to him right away, to have him want me. It was wonderful that morning!

'Over the next few weeks I was all laughter and energy in front of Peter but dived into depression as soon as he went out or wasn't there. I would burst into tears when I was at work or went out shopping. I didn't want to get up in the morning and I couldn't sleep at night. I couldn't eat and became agoraphobic. I eventually went to the doctor and he asked me if there was anything that might have triggered the depression. When I told him, I could see that he was shocked and this only served to make the situation worse. He knew Peter as we both used the same practice. He put me on Prozac and referred me to a counsellor. He thought that it was strange that I had not exploded at Peter and I suppose he was right.

'I carried on like this for two awful months. Disgusting as it is I became used to making love to Peter knowing that he would be making love to Greg the following day. I had given up – the situation had beaten me! I felt that I had to 'win' the competition with

Greg and found myself putting more into our sex life. It was the only thing I did put any effort into!

'Eventually I realised I had to face the problem or end up in an institution. I needed Peter out of my life. I decided to confront him in a calm and controlled way when he returned from a three-day flight. As he walked through the front door I came out of the kitchen and looked at him coldly. My eyes filled with tears and his filled with fear. We both knew what this was all about. Suddenly I lost it. I flew at Peter and punched him squarely on the nose. He fell to the floor and his nose was pouring with blood. I was shocked at what I had done whilst feeling a great emotional release.

'All the pain and the hurt – everything I had kept to myself – came flooding out. Peter burst into tears on the floor and started saying, over and over again, that he was sorry. I couldn't speak but I suddenly realised that Peter was hurting as well. So in the middle of the kitchen floor, which was now covered in Peter's blood, I held him.

'I felt ashamed for what I had done but was still angry because I had been robbed of the scene I'd planned before the punch. We made a cup of tea and then settled on the sofa for the long overdue 'talk' on the subject.

'Peter told me that it all started as a bit of a giggle. The two of them had gone out one night and Greg had taken him to a gay bar 'for a laugh'.

Every time they went out after that they ended up in the same places. One night, after they'd had a lot to drink, Greg had suggested getting a room in town because it was too late to catch a train home. Peter said Greg had planned this but it didn't wash with me.

'As Peter told his story I burst into tears. He put his arms around me, kissed me and we made love. Although I wanted to, I knew that this would be the last time it would ever happen.

'I confronted Greg at my parent's house. I made sure that my mum and dad weren't in the room because I couldn't bear to have them find out. Greg was getting redder by the minute. Apparently, Peter had called him and told him that I knew, so he was very embarrassed when I turned up out of the blue. He just looked at me and shrugged his shoulders and gave me a pathetic smile. It was all I could do to stop myself from punching him.

'I swore at him under my breath. He became angry and we started calling each other names. All of a sudden we were going at it like cat and dog. I hit Greg with the magazine rack but he grabbed hold of my arms. I screamed. When my mum came running in Greg let go of me. As I stormed out I could hear my parents yelling at Greg to 'stop upsetting your sister'. If only they had known the truth, they would have done a little more than shout!

'When I returned home Greg had already phoned Peter to tell him about the scene at my mum's house. He said he thought he ought to find somewhere else to live. A few weeks later I came back from a flight to find a note. It said something about him being weak and being sorry and that maybe this was the best thing to do all round — all that old rubbish! I was relieved he had gone but felt that he should have been more of a man about it.

'My parents still know nothing about Greg and Peter and that's the way I want to keep it. I have another boyfriend now but I will never again be able to trust a man fully. I haven't seen my brother more than twice since that afternoon and don't intend to.

———————————

'If you do pursue your partner you may also misconstrue a situation. In the following case study Jessie saw something that was not what it appeared to be:

———————————

Jessie was convinced that her husband was cheating on her and followed him on several occasions but saw nothing suspicious.

One afternoon, however, she saw her husband enter a bar with an attractive young woman. When he returned home later, she began shouting and accusing him of all kinds of unfaithful behaviour.

It turned out that Jessie's husband was planning a surprise party for their wedding anniversary and the young woman in the bar was the caterer!

Equally, you may follow your partner on occasions when they do not meet their lover, wrongly convincing you of their innocence.

My advice is that you should not follow your partner under any circumstances. Should you wish to take this course of action, use a reputable private detective agency or ask a friend, remembering that they may misinterpret situations or react badly in just the same way as you.

You are much better advised to lay a trap for your partner.

Setting Traps

If you keep up with the news, you will know that this technique has backfired badly on the police in recent years. Suspects have been able to argue that they were unfairly 'led on' by the police and that there were innocent explanations for their behaviour. Just as the victims in these situations have frequently chosen to sue the police afterwards, you may find yourself with an extremely angry partner. If they haven't broken the trust of the relationship, they may feel that you have!

Car Traps

Preparation:

1) Record the mileage.

2) Clean the car inside and out, not forgetting the ashtray, door pockets and glove box.

3) Use the 'matchstick in the seatbelt holder' technique described on page 67.

4) Lightly dust the back seats, carpets and front seat carpets with a non-scented talc. The best way to do this is by pouring talc into your hand and blowing gently over the top. If you follow the directions properly you should achieve an even spread of talc that is invisible in the street light. Repeat the procedure with the door handles on the passenger doors.

5) Polish the windows.

6) Invest in a voice activated tape-recorder and place it under the passenger seat. It will remain dormant until the car is used. You should test the recording level at which the machine is set so that it is not activated by the sound of the engine.

7) Ask your partner where they are going.

8) Ask your partner what they will be doing.

9) Ask your partner who they will be going out with.

What to do next:
When your partner returns home:

1) Check the mileage.

2) Check the talc deposits for any disturbance. This will help you determine whether your partner had any passengers on board.

3) Check the inside of the car for finger and foot prints. Breathe on the glass before you check for prints as this will make the marks more visible.

4) Look for the matchstick in the seatbelt holder.

5) Search the car as outlined in the 'car checking' section on page 90.

6) Listen to the voice-activated tape recorder.

Record all of your findings and do not forget to add the details of your partner's alibi. Don't do anything else, however good your evidence seems. I will tell you how to proceed later on in 'putting it all together'.

_____

Karen suspected her husband Mike of having an affair. He was a keep-fit fanatic and went to the gym four nights a week. Despite the fact that he went on his own and claimed that he trained alone and came home alone, Karen was sure he was seeing someone else on at least one of these nights. So, to test her theory, she tried putting a matchstick in the passenger seatbelt holder of Mike's car.

On Mondays, Wednesdays and Thursdays the matchstick was untouched and remained lodged in the seatbelt. However on Tuesdays Karen would always find the matchstick on the passenger floor carpet.

Karen enlisted the help of a friend one Tuesday evening. They followed Mike to the gym and waited outside. Karen was just about to give up, assuming that he was exercising as normal, when he reappeared hand-in-hand with a woman. Karen followed them to the car park where the couple got into Mike's car. She remembers praying that it would all be innocent and that Mike was simply giving the woman a lift home.

Mike drove his mystery passenger to a bar, however. As Karen looked through the window she felt stupid and a little tacky. However she soon lost her inhibitions when she saw Mike kissing the woman in an unambiguous manner at the bar. Karen stormed in and caused a scene. Mike and Karen are now divorced.

Telephone Trap

Does your partner often answer the telephone only to tell you that it was a 'wrong number'? Or does the caller often hang up when you answer the telephone?

Your partner may be receiving calls from the other man or woman at home. Dangerous as this may sound, many cheating couples do contact each other this way, perhaps using codes.

Next time it happens – whether to your partner or you – discreetly find out the number of the last caller. In the United Kingdom the way to do this is to dial 1471 when the call is finished. If the recorded message gives a number write it down. Obviously if you are told that the 'caller withheld their number' this will give grounds for suspicion. The caller will have dialled 141 before the call (to withhold their identity) or phoned from overseas.

If you can get a number, use the directory enquiry service to find the area from which the call originated. Do this each and every time the telephone goes dead or there is a 'wrong number'. It will become obvious, after only a few calls, whether the same person is calling your number regularly.

Keep a record of dates, times and the behaviour of your partner immediately after each call. Do they find an excuse to 'pop out' afterwards or do they start an argument in a bid to reach the 'storming out' stage?

I have already described the technique by which, immediately after a suspect call, you can press the record button on a tape recorder and find an excuse to leave the house, telling your partner exactly how long you are going to be away. If their lover *has* just called then chances are your partner will want to call them back when you leave the house.

When you play the tape back, you may hear your partner make a call, but say nothing. Perhaps they have tried to phone the other man or woman at home without knowing that the earlier incoming call came from a different number. Should this occur, invent some reason why you were trying to call your partner and explain that the phone was engaged when you were trying to get through. Your partner will offer an excuse for using the telephone. If your telephone has one, press the re-dial button. If the person your partner claims to have called answers – no problem. If you find that the call didn't come from the place your partner put forward then be suspicious and write down all the details.

If, on the other hand, a stranger answers, then you may have found a flaw in the story. Remember, the receiver of your re-dialled call may repeat their number upon answering. Be prepared with a pen and paper because you will only have one chance.

Look at your past telephone bills for that number. Apart from offering clear corroboration to your suspicions, it will show you how long this affair (if it is such) has been going on.

Bank Account Trap

At some point in your investigations you will have a strong suspicion that your partner is going to meet their lover.

Should they be planning to use cash to fund their indiscretions, thereby avoiding suspicious entries on their bank and credit card statements, you can set a very effective trap, especially if you hold a joint account with your partner.

Empty the account 3–4 days before the likely rendezvous. You will have to find a good excuse in keeping with your lifestyle. On the day or night of their tryst, your partner will attempt to withdraw money but will be refused. Their only option may then be to use a credit card.

When they return you will probably bear the brunt of their frustration but you will also know that they tried to withdraw cash. If they don't tell you, ask them.

In the following weeks your partner may begin to show an unhealthy interest in the mail. They may want to access the credit card statement before you do.

There follows a case study which shows a classic – and original – trap in action:

Emma is married to Bob. She has an infirm mother whom she cares for each weekend. Emma has to go to her mother's house on Friday night and cannot return home until the day-nurse arrives on Monday morning. Bob told her he was lonely on his own at the weekend and would spend Friday to Sunday at his brother's or at his friend's house. Emma became suspicious when, without thinking, she called her home one weekend from her mother's house.

As she finished dialling she realised that nobody would be there but, before she could put the phone down, she heard the engaged tone. This was odd, so she dialled again with the same result. Bob was supposed to be at his brother's flat and they didn't have an answerphone, so how could the telephone be engaged?

Why was Bob at home when he claimed to be away? Emma came up with an ingenious trap. All the heating, cooking and hot water in their house was powered by electricity alone. One Friday night Emma took a reading of the electric meter before she left for her mother's house. When she returned on Monday morning she took another reading. The discrepancy between the two was so large that someone had to have been using the house over the weekend. But when she asked Bob what he had been doing, he said that he was at his brother's as usual.

Emma kept a record of the electricity usage at her home each weekend for the next six weeks and a

pattern soon emerged. Every other week the meter
reading was 30 to 50 units higher than it should have
been. Emma smelled a rat and, on the next weekend
when she could predict a high use of electricity, she
returned home early on Saturday night, paying the
day-nurse to care for her mother.

As she went through the front door Bob called
out from the bath: 'Is that you darling?' When Emma
answered in the affirmative and asked him what he
was doing in the house, Bob jumped out of the bath
and started giving her a lame excuse. He tried to convince Emma to go back to her mother's as quickly as
possible. It was obvious to Emma that he was expecting somebody else.

Ten minutes later, Emma heard a key in the door
and Bob ran to 'deal' with the situation. It was too
late! Bob's lover (who had her own key) let herself in
and Bob could only stand there red-faced. As soon as
his lover realised what was going on, she ran out
of the house.

Bob tried to lie his way out but Emma showed
him her record of the electric meter readings and
told him exactly when his lover had been to their
house. Faced with all this evidence, Bob confessed
and begged for Emma's forgiveness. They had a very
difficult reconciliation period but managed to talk
to each other and to work through the problems
within the marriage. Emma gave Bob another

chance and, as far as we know, Bob has remained
faithful ever since.

────────────

This shows how effective traps can be in the search for
truth. But be careful. If they are poorly thought out or not
'set' in as systematic and realistic manner as this example,
they will not only go wrong but could backfire on you.

Remember too to try to keep your sense of objectivity. Fingerprints on the inside of the car window do not
mean your partner is having an affair, merely that *someone* has used the passenger seat.

Chapter 6

Your Conclusions, Your Confrontation

When you have gathered good quality data from as many sources as possible you will need to try to bring it all together into a coherent picture. Your dossier should have at least 10 pieces of hard evidence and 15 pieces of circumstantial evidence (active and passive signals) before you proceed to any confrontation.

Processing the Evidence in Your Dossier

The evidence may go back as far as six months. The entries that were made at that time may still need to be cross referenced with, say, recent telephone bills or bank account/credit card statements. Do not act until you have gathered all of this evidence and recorded it.

Your dossier will probably run from 20 to 30 pages and will contain a number of entries for each incident, with a space left at the bottom of the page for cross references or other evidence that may have come to light long after the initial event. Fill in all the blank spaces and record all the inconsistencies.

You should now produce a condensed version of your dossier running to 10 to 15 pages. This is the document with which you will (if you choose) confront your unfaithful partner, so include only the most damning of evidence and leave out irrelevant or unclear entries. Use another exercise book and, starting from page one in your dossier, document all alibis given for strange behaviour against the hard evidence proving otherwise. Don't forget to include times and dates. Now add circumstantial evidence such as car mileage/car search material. This part of the dossier should take up approximately five to eight pages of condensed evidence.

Next, detail telephone and/or letter information, including all telephone numbers, addresses and names. This should take up another two to three pages.

Lastly detail all other stray pieces of information you may have discovered along the way. These should fit into either 'circumstantial' or 'real' evidence, not just be slipped in at the end. Any stray piece of evidence should be given a definite place in your incident report.

Preparing for the Confrontation

Now that you have a complete and concise document you can consider your next step. If you have performed the detection techniques outlined in this guide correctly, your partner should be oblivious to the 'bomb' with which you are about to hit them.

Can *you* remember what you were doing six weeks ago and, if you had to tell a lie, what it was? I doubt it!

By now your partner will have long forgotten the alibis and escape stories that they told you all those weeks and months ago, thinking they had got away with it. The bank statements, suspect parking tickets and fictitious friends will be indistinguishable from one another.

It is you who has the multiple pieces of hard evidence and can outline the movements they have long forgotten. If and when you confront your partner, they will be presented with so much evidence that even the most accomplished liar should crumble.

The Confrontation

There will never be a good time for the confrontation because it is never a pleasant task. But there are 'worse' and 'better' times. Try to be on familiar territory. Make sure that your partner does not have a good excuse to escape; for example, don't confront him 10 minutes before a friend is due to pick him up. Christmas, birthdays and the occasions of other social and family events are to be avoided at all costs. Never confront someone when you are feeling angry, resentful, or violent – perhaps if you have just discovered some damning evidence. Give yourself time to calm down and behave in a rational manner. Alcohol for 'Dutch courage' is a no-no.

You will need to be as sure as you'll ever be of your partner's infidelity. Make sure you won't be interrupted. Turn the telephone off. Create a calm environment as much for your own sake as for the purposes of the confrontation.

Before you confront your partner you must consider the consequences. Ask yourself:

- Why do I want to confront my partner right now?

- Am I ready for the trauma that the confrontation will cause? Am I strong enough at the moment? (Consider everything else that is happening in your life.)

- Do I want to retrieve the relationship after the confrontation? Will my partner want to continue?

- Is either of us likely to be hostile or violent during the confrontation? Will this be controllable?

- Is there another way of handling the situation?

- Will friends and family support me?

- How will a changed domestic situation (e.g. children, work, finances) affect my lifestyle?

As you can see, the subject of infidelity touches all aspects of your life. Give yourself time to cool off and think about the future.

Undoubtedly, after you have confronted your partner, your relationship will change. Several of my interviewees had spent many months collecting evidence but told me that their partner's infidelity wasn't real to them until it was actually admitted. They were hit by waves of jealousy, resentment, foolishness, disgust and terrible disappointment. Whether you try again or bring things to an end, your life will never be the same.

Should you eventually try to be reconciled with your partner, your conduct now could be the blueprint for the whole reconciliation process. So don't confront your partner in a hostile or aggressive manner, perhaps after you have just discovered some damning evidence. Avoid saying or doing something you will come to regret with the benefit of hindsight. Don't hurl your evidence at your partner in a random and frenzied manner. There will be a horrific argument and the impact you could have caused by delivering all your evidence in a clear and concise way will be lost.

However, the confrontation does give you the chance to sweep away all the emotional deadwood. Now and in the future there will be occasions when you will be wracked with anger and jealousy over your partner's past indiscretions. This is perfectly normal. Do not bottle anything up! If you need to talk, then talk, either to your partner or a close friend.

If you let a friend into the truth of your situation don't tell them details that you would not want them to know under normal circumstances. Later, if you find yourself getting closer to your partner, it will be embarrassing for you to have a friend around who knows so much about both of you. In these situations the one-time cheated partner usually drops the friend in favour of their reformed partner. Many friendships have been lost this way so try to exercise some restraint.

If you split from your partner don't expect to be free of the bad feelings. You may think you are making a new start but you are still mourning the end of a relationship and coping with betrayal. You will probably feel inadequate, lonely, afraid and angry. These are quite normal feelings. Nobody should ever tell you it will be easy!

You may be wondering how important your evidence will be in the event of divorce and custody proceedings. Regrettably I am not qualified to tell you, especially since the law on these matters is often revised and differs substantially from country to country. Consult a lawyer either before you confront your partner or even earlier in your investigation if you think you may want to take your findings into court.

In the following case study Nathalie suspected her boyfriend Tim of infidelity. When she went to visit him, however, it was not to confront him but to confess to her own infidelity.

———————————

Nathalie (23) had been going out with Tim (25) for 18 months. She felt the 'honeymoon' period of the relationship was over and that Tim was beginning to lose interest. She was sure he was seeing other women and it was upsetting her. He was attractive, with his own flat, and she suspected it was easy for him to 'play away'.

One evening a friend of Nathalie's, Charlotte, stayed the night following her return from a four-month stay in the United States. In her months away she had turned from being a slightly overweight sallow-skinned student into a stunning and healthy looking woman. As the evening progressed and the two girls prepared to go out, Nathalie had plenty of chance to admire her friend's body and it excited her in a way she had never felt before.

Since they shared a bed that night, Nathalie toyed with the idea of waking her friend and telling her. She resisted the temptation, only to have Charlotte tell her the next day that she had discovered she was bisexual whilst she was away. The two made love and, within a couple of days, Charlotte returned to share the flat with Nathalie.

Nathalie: 'There was still Tim. I didn't really want to see him because I was more interested in Charlotte, but I didn't want to give him up either. The question of whether he was 'playing away' was still very much on my mind too. There's this quote in *The Picture of Dorian Gray* about how we'd throw more things away if we weren't afraid that someone else would pick them up. I suppose that's how I felt.

'Charlotte and I were out one night, having a few drinks, when I suddenly decided it was time to confront Tim. Charlotte tried to talk me out of it, saying that a drunken confrontation in the middle of the night really wasn't the best strategy, but I ignored her and got a taxi to his place. She refused to come with me and went back to my flat.

'I arrived at Tim's full of anger, expecting to find him full of apologies for his lack of interest in me during the past month. But then I saw an ambulance outside his flat. It turned out that Leon, Tim's friend, had had an epileptic fit. Tim was drunk and upstairs in bed. Jules, another of Tim's friends, stood on the stairs with a girl. I didn't take any notice of her as I barged past and went into Tim's bedroom.

'His landlord, who lived in the flat downstairs, was in the room trying to drag Tim out of bed, yelling at him to pack his bags and get out. Eventually he agreed to come back in the morning when things were a little calmer. I was sitting on the bed stroking Tim's hair when the girl I had seen on the stairs walked into the bedroom and started shouting in some foreign language. I think she was Italian. Tim said she was a friend of Jules' but when I went down the stairs and asked him to get rid of her, he said: "She's got nothing to do with me. She's with Tim." Then it dawned on me what I'd walked into. I went back into the bedroom and demanded to know whether Tim had made love to the girl. He grinned back at me, slurred "of course" and started giggling.

'I sat on his chest and pummelled his face. All he could do was laugh which only made me more angry. So, I just said to him: "You needn't look so smug. I've been having a bit on the side myself." When he finally registered what I'd said he demanded to know who "he" was. "He?" I said. "What makes you so sure it's a "he"? After your sorry show as a man do you really think I'd be desperate to take up with another one?" Then I told him everything.

'Tim came round the next morning demanding more answers. He could only remember that we'd had a massive row. He wanted to make up. I repeated what I'd said and we had a huge argument. Only this time Charlotte got dragged into it too. She was really embarrassed and quite angry with me for the way I handled the situation. I'm not proud of it. She was right when she said that I used her to get at Tim but I was with her because she appealed to me, on many levels, in more ways than Tim did. It could have been a man or a woman, but it happened to be a woman. I didn't see Tim again.'

By contrast, Kiki's controlled confrontation with Brett is a much better example of how to approach a suspected unfaithful partner. As you will see, she remains in control at all times.

Kiki (38) has been married to Brett (42) for 15 years. They have three children aged four, six and nine. Kiki looks after the children at home and Brett is an engineer who frequently works away from home.

Kiki suspected Brett of having an affair when he returned home from an overnight work trip smelling of alcohol and perfume. Over a period of three months she compiled an evidence dossier, detailing all of Brett's movements, alibis, credit information... etc. Eventually she presented Brett with 10 pages of undeniable proof of his adultery. She decided to record the confrontation in case it was required as evidence in a divorce case and has kindly allowed me to quote it in part:

K: Could we have a little talk please Brett?

B: Yeah sure – what's the problem?

K: Well I'm going to be direct with you. I have a good reason for thinking that you are not being entirely honest with me about your work trips.

B: Oh yes. What's brought this on then?

K: Well, several months ago you came home smelling of booze and somebody else's perfume and it made me suspicious.

B: Well that's a load of b******s. I go to work to pay for all this and...

K: If I can just stop you there you'll see that it's not just a feeling. I have some evidence.

B: What is all this? Evidence? Has that soppy sister of yours been talking you into hating me again?

K: It's got nothing to do with her. Remember when you went away to work on that Scottish project a couple of months ago?

B: Yes. That was that shopping centre that we
were working on. You know where...

K: I know nothing of the sort. Your bank account
statement says that you were eating a meal in
London the night you were supposed to be in
Scotland. So what have you got to say to that?

B: Oh that er... I gave Dave my Switch card
because he needed some money to take some girl out.

K: So you gave Dave your Switch card and he
forged your signature – is that what you're telling me?

B: Yes. We always do that kind of thing for each
other – I put myself out for my friends, you know
that.

K: Did Dave also use your card for the hotel and
the drinks in the night-club as well?

B: Look, I've told you. We do these kind of things
for each other – and what are you doing looking at
my bank statements anyway? Is this the f***ing
Spanish Inquisition or what?

K: Please stop swearing, it's not like you normally.
Right then, for a start they are our bank statements –
it's a joint account remember. And secondly, if you
have nothing to hide then you won't mind me looking will you?

B: I've got nothing to hide. Carry on.

K: If Dave used your card for his London jaunt,
then what did you use for the Scottish trip?

B: I used the Access card and some cash that
I took from the hole in the wall before I went.

K: The credit card statement shows no sign of being used in Scotland during that time.

B: Look, I've had enough of this c**p. You've gone mad woman. If you don't...

K: ... And if you had taken cash we'd be able to see the withdrawal on the statement – look, nothing.

Kiki had photocopied the bank statements and circled the relevant entries in preparation for the confrontation.

B: Well, that's obviously a mistake on the bank's part.

K: Where were you Brett?

B: I was in Scotland. I told you.

K: If you were in Scotland why weren't you paid the working away allowance that month?

B: I was paid the working...

K: Oh no you weren't because it's not on that month's salary details.

B: So you've been looking at my f***ing wage slips as well have you?

K: If you've got nothing to hide then you should-n't mind me looking should you?

B: Stop saying that. I told you, I've got nothing to hide...

Kiki then questioned Brett about five other occa-sions when he said he had been working away and was not. This illustrates the importance of having multiple pieces of hard evidence. One bad explana-tion might be excusable. But five? I think not!

Brett continued to protest his innocence. The more he realised the seriousness of the situation, the more he denied the evidence against him – the 'shoplifter syndrome' I described earlier. It is typical of unfaithful partners and explains why Kiki had to confront him with so many damning situations.

Brett began to crack when Kiki gave him the name and telephone number of someone she knew he had been calling secretly for some time. (Kiki had used the telephone techniques outlined in this book.) Eventually Brett broke down in tears and admitted to Kiki that he had been seeing another woman for over a year.

Kiki decided to give Brett another chance. Sadly, she later discovered that her husband was having another affair and divorced him. She has since remarried and retained custody of her three children.

So you have brought matters to a head and must now live with the consequences. If you wish to try to rebuild your relationship you should probably seek independent help from a recognised counselling service. You can find the appropriate telephone numbers in the telephone directory or by calling a telephone information service.

With or without help it is essential that all the details of your partner's infidelity are brought into the open. No amount of shouting, talking or counselling will help the relationship to progress without the truth, no matter how upsetting it may be.

Then the hard work begins. You may experience overwhelming feelings of possessiveness and feel that you cannot trust your partner in any way. You will even find it hard to believe that the cheat really wants to try again. You may also lose your self-esteem and blame the cheat for your negative view of yourself.

In her excellent book *The Relate Guide to Staying Together*, Susan Quilliam lists three principles by which you should try to abide if you want to try to save your relationship:

First, Quilliam recommends: 'Resist the temptation to punish each other.' The strong emotions associated with infidelity make it very difficult to forgive. You may take such pleasure in 'punishing' the reformed cheat that you find yourself on the end of a backlash of anger from them.

The second principle she stresses is, 'Understand why the affair happened.' How much do we really know about our partners? Talking about the reasons for their infidelity can often open up a Pandora's box of unresolved problems in your relationship – problems which have crept in over a period of years. Maybe there was not enough excitement. Or the sex was boring and infrequent. Or one of you was too busy or too ill-equipped to express themselves emotionally.

Last, she asks: 'Change the recognised problems within the relationship so that infidelity doesn't occur again.' At this point you may need some help from the relationship counselling services I already mentioned.

I met several couples who had chosen to make their relationships more 'open' after one partner had been unfaithful. These relationships always seemed to be under strain. Some individuals – particularly men – were using them as an excuse to look for someone new. In several cases their female partners had then gone off with one of their new lovers! In my view an open relationship is not a relationship.

And forget revenge. It will make a strained situation 10 times worse. Channel your vengeful thoughts into positive action. The best revenge is to get yourself together and show your partner that you are your own person, whether or not you choose to stay with them. You've been the victim of a cheat, but there is life afterwards!

Afterword

I sincerely hope that this book has been of use to you and that your detective work proves your partner to have been a faithful mate. You will then at least be able to continue the relationship with honesty and trust.

If, on the other hand, your fears have been born out, you can make an informed decision about what you want from the future based on the truth.

All the techniques outlined in *To Catch a Cheat* are tried and tested and have been gathered over a two year period. The research involved talking to both the cheats and the cheated.

I am always looking for unusual incidents of infidelity or sexual obsession for use in further publications. I would also invite you to send your comments and personal stories to the address below:

Jim Richardson
P.O. Box 275
Sevenoaks
Kent TN13 1ZD